Praise for *Communicate with Mastery*

"*Communicate with Mastery* is an entertaining and practical guide to presenting and communicating. JD exposes our issues with confidence as communicators and reveals a pathway out of the darkness of doubt. With over twenty years of practical classroom experience poured into an easy-to-read guide, JD provides readers with the tools to engage any audience, tailor impactful messages, and navigate any communication challenge."

Stephen J. Mellas
Principal at a Global Asset Management Firm
Adjunct Professor of Management Communication, NYU Stern

"In this engaging book, JD Schramm provides us actionable advice for how to communicate more effectively based on years of teaching and consulting. He explains how to understand your audience, find your voice, tell compelling stories, and communicate with authenticity. Schramm argues that there's no such thing as a perfect presentation or report. We can always do better, if we are willing to seek feedback, listen actively, and iterate often. This book is a true masterpiece on persuading your audience!"

Michael Roberto
Author, *Unlocking Creativity*
Trustee Professor of Management, Bryant University

"My clients and students often ask me: what's the difference between a confident leader and an arrogant leader? My answer: confident leaders share. *Communicating with Mastery* embraces sharing as fundamental to any leader's effectiveness, and every page embodies that approach: *Communicating with Mastery* overflows with strategies; some of these strategies are brand new, others are time-tested, but every word of this book is *fresh* for the world that awaits us, a world that serves as the crucible through which existing and evolving leaders will test their mettle. Leaders of all kinds—early, evolving and established—will benefit from this book."

Tim Flood
Managing Director, Management Communication Association
Associate Professor, UNC Kenan-Flagler School of Business

"A straightforward and approachable guide for anyone seeking to improve his or her communication skills. JD has both the expertise and perhaps more critically, the emotional understanding required to personally connect with any current or future leader reading this book."

Mike Lewis
Author, *When to Jump: If the Job You Have Isn't The Life You Want*

"Many authors encourage leaders to be authentic communicators, but JD Schramm goes further and provides frameworks and actions to bring about authentic communication. I've relied on many of his techniques in my own presentations and am pleased that he has now captured it all in one place so others can benefit from his insights too."

Erin Uritus
CEO, Out & Equal Workplace Advocates

"In *Communicate with Mastery*, JD Schramm provides us with a 'best practice Bible' that addresses a vast array of communication challenges leaders can expect to confront in their careers. The author resists prescribing a one size fits all solution, and instead helps the reader look inward to find the powerful, authentic messages that will resonate with their audiences. Nowhere is this wisdom more apt than in the pages JD devotes to communications challenges that most often befall minority groups that face systemic discrimination and bias. JD urges leaders in the LGBTQ community, for example, to avoid the hiding and passing techniques that are commonly relied up and instead to build trust through transparency, vulnerability and honesty. JD's big lesson is that successful professional communications are ultimately based on robust and authentic personal connections."

John Tedstrom
Founder, NextGen Leaders
CEO, Tedstrom Associates

"In his engaging and relatable style, JD synthesizes the most powerful/relevant ideas in communication and coaching. *Communicate with Mastery* gives leaders the tools to develop an authentic style and powerful presence. Mastery of communication is an ongoing process, and JD provides the motivation and strategies for lifelong improvement that you will use every day."

Molly Epstein
Professor in the Practice of Organization and Management
Goizueta Business School at Emory University

BY **JD SCHRAMM**, ED.D

WITH **KARA LEVY**

COMMUNICATE

WITH

MASTERY

HOW TO SPEAK WITH
CONVICTION AND
WRITE FOR IMPACT

WILEY

Published by John Wiley & Sons, Inc., Hoboken, New Jersey.
Published simultaneously in Canada.

For general information on our other products and services or for technical support, please contact our Customer Care Department within the United States at (800) 762–2974, outside the United States at (317) 572–3993 or fax (317) 572–4002.

Wiley publishes in a variety of print and electronic formats and by print-on-demand. Some material included with standard print versions of this book may not be included in e-books or in print-on-demand. If this book refers to media such as a CD or DVD that is not included in the version you purchased, you may download this material at http://booksupport.wiley.com. For more information about Wiley products, visit www.wiley.com.

Library of Congress Cataloging-in-Publication Data:

Names: Schramm, J. D., author. | Levy, Kara, author.
Title: Communicate with mastery : how to speak with conviction and write
   for impact / by JD Schramm, Ed.D, with Kara Levy.
Description: Hoboken, New Jersey : John Wiley & Sons, Inc., [2020] |
   Includes bibliographical references and index.
Identifiers: LCCN 2019045131 (print) | LCCN 2019045132 (ebook) | ISBN
   9781119550099 (hardback) | ISBN 9781119550143 (adobe pdf) | ISBN
   9781119550167 (epub)
Subjects: LCSH: Communication in management. | Business communication. |
   Leadership.
Classification: LCC HD30.3 .S365 2020 (print) | LCC HD30.3 (ebook) | DDC
   658.4/5—dc23
LC record available at https://lccn.loc.gov/2019045131
LC ebook record available at https://lccn.loc.gov/2019045132

Cover image: © Getty Images | JAYK7
Cover design: Paul McCarthy

Printed in the United States of America

V10016315_121319

To Ken, Toby, Roma, and Joshua—My greatest teachers on how to communicate with greater mastery. The best mirrors we have for our communication are those with whom we spend the most amount of time; for me, that's my husband, Ken, and our three kids. I regret that this book has taken some of our precious time from one another, yet I'm committed to being even more present to you using the lessons I learned and now share here.—JDS

To my past and current students at Stanford, Columbia, and NYU—Thank you for the privilege of being your teacher, but know that it exists as truly a two-way relationship. I learned from you as well; sometimes even more than I provided. May we keep the relationship alive. —JDS

To my mentors, colleagues, and the inspiring leaders who entrust me with their communication—With gratitude for all that I learn from you every day.—KL

CONTENTS

FOREWORD

Early in my career, I traveled to Claremont College, where I got advice from the father of modern management, the late Peter Drucker. That advice has since served me well: *"Build on your strengths; and make your weaknesses irrelevant."* This was the opposite of what I was doing. I was working to address my limitations, and, in so doing, I was ignoring my natural abilities, sometimes laboring toward mediocrity.

Every year, Graham Weaver, founder of Alpine Investors, comes to a second-year MBA class that I teach at Stanford. One of the most powerful lessons he leaves with students is a simple metaphor: *"Water your flowers and cut your weeds."* It's another version of the advice that Drucker gave to an aspiring young leader many years earlier. Powerful as it may be, it is counterintuitive advice to most of us working on a portfolio of problems and opportunities.

The same wisdom applies to our efforts to communicate effectively. Many books give high-level encouragement for powerful and effective communications; yet few instruct leaders on how to build on their strengths as a communicator and make their weaknesses irrelevant. The book you hold in your hands provides that path forward.

My friend and colleague JD Schramm has captured in one place the heart of what he's taught to our students at Stanford about writing and speaking as a leader. Not only has he opened up his classroom to all of us, but he has also included interviews with the legion of coaches and instructors he has cultivated at Stanford.

When I consider the wide range of skills required of leaders today, many of them boil down to clear thinking and clear communication. This book will provide you the insights necessary to "grow your own communication flowers and cut away the weeds" from your writing and speaking.

Enjoy the journey JD has in store for you in the pages ahead.

Joel Peterson
Chairman of the Board, JetBlue Airways

INTRODUCTION

Over the past decade at Stanford's Graduate School of Business (GSB), we've developed a practice of communication coaching that empowers our MBA students to communicate effectively and authentically. We encourage them to journey from uncertainty, to competence, to expertise, and ultimately to mastery.

I struggle with that first term, "uncertainty," because when our students show up each fall, they are in a wide range of places regarding experience, facility with communication techniques, and confidence. Some are terrified at the prospect of speaking in public or sharing their writing; others have practiced these skills for years while working in consulting, banking, or private equity, and feel they have nothing to learn from the coaches and instructors. Others still have already published books or delivered talks at Davos or TED. To imagine a "one size fits all" approach to communication is folly. Peers at other institutions have told me stories of how hard it is to teach communication in a required course to such a diverse population.

So instead of adding to the core requirements at the GSB, we went a different route: we decided to tailor our communication offerings as fully as we could. By taking this approach, our offerings became sought-after electives with long waiting lists. From zero offerings in the fall of 2007, as of the 2019 writing of this book we have 20 sections of communication courses taught by five different lecturers. In addition, our tenured colleagues are teaching another 20 sections of related courses like Acting with Power, Selling, and

Difficult Conversations, none of which existed in 2007. Year after year, students report that their training in communication has been key to their success at the GSB and beyond. Now, in this book, you can learn the elements of our "secret sauce for success" to build up your own communication skills (or those of your employees) without the time and expense of a Stanford MBA. (Of course, there are other benefits to this degree . . . so we still encourage you to apply!)

We quite purposefully used the term "mastery" in describing our work at the GSB and in this book. It's derived from Dan Pink's work on motivation in *Drive: The Surprising Truth About What Motivates Us*, where he examines the three elements of motivation: autonomy, mastery, and purpose. He defines mastery as "the desire to get better and better at something that matters" (111). He further clarifies that mastery is an asymptote, the straight line that a curve approaches but never quite reaches (126–127; Figure I.1).

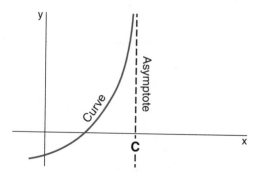

Figure I.1 Geometric refresh: The image of an asymptote

At Stanford we have encouraged our students to seek mastery in communication as an unattainable aspiration (Figure I.2). There is no such thing as a perfect email, talk, book, or presentation. Each aspect of leadership communication can always be improved. With each successive iteration we hope leaders will improve their ability to communicate, knowing that perfect never comes.

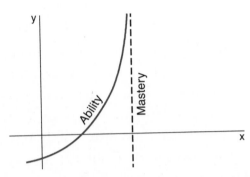

Figure I.2 Leaders approach mastery in communication

Our secret sauce to empowering young leaders (and you, our readers) is five-fold:

INDIVIDUALITY: Communication development is an individual sport. No two leaders communicate in exactly the same way. Good communication development means doubling down on your strengths as well as adding extra tools to your communication toolbox.

RELEVANCE: When leaders write or speak, they should choose topics that matter to them (to the extent possible). The more that passion, interest, or applicability drive the message, the better it will be.

ITERATION: Continual iteration (with feedback) is the key to improvement. Practice means failing, succeeding, trying new approaches, soliciting and integrating feedback, and then repeating.

FEEDBACK: Leaders learn on both sides of the microscope. It's as valuable to give feedback as to receive it—and both of these sides of the coin are a skill you can learn.

STAKES: When you increase the visibility and reach of a piece, you increase commitment to making it great. Raise the stakes to encourage the best from yourself.

Let's dive into each of these elements in greater depth.

Individuality

Today's business school assignments contain an inordinate number of group assignments. An optimist might say we are committed to helping students learn how to work in teams before they go out to lead teams. A realist (or a pessimist!) might say it's easier for a professor to grade 12 team assignments than 72 individual papers. Both perspectives have some merit. But in the discipline of communication, we need to hone our individual skills as writers and speakers.

The best business reports are written with one voice (probably with input and edits from a team), but with singular leadership. To build skills effectively, leaders must write on their own and speak on their own. When you can tailor your work to your existing skills and talents, the outcome will be more efficient for you and more engaging for your audience. Certainly I deliver "lectures" to large groups at Stanford and elsewhere, but they're very interactive—if the members of the class or audience want to improve, they need to stand up and speak, or sit down and write. I also task students with self-reflection on almost every piece they write or deliver. This process of individual self-critique requires them to be thoughtful about what truly worked or didn't work in their talk or paper and, most importantly, to commit to goals for improvement before the next opportunity to communicate.

Relevance

That leads us to relevance—starting with the relevance of the assigned material. So often in other B-school classes students read and write endlessly about case studies of CEOs (usually male, though increasingly more diverse) and the firms they established or turned around. Case write-ups are a good way to learn strategy or finance or marketing, but not to learn writing. We have found that if students can write about material that matters to them personally, they will be more engaged and take the coaching much more seriously. If I provide edits on a deck for start-ups students are leading (or will launch after graduation), they are keen to understand every correction and suggestion. If they can speak persuasively about a cause they embrace or an issue they face, the presentation will be much more compelling. Admittedly, those of us who are no longer in school know that from time to time, we do have to write and speak on topics that aren't our particular passion. That's life. It can also happen in our classroom, but the more we can reduce it, the more our future leaders will stay engaged.

Iteration

All published writers and successful keynote speakers know that their work only gets better with revision—often revisions, plural. Rarely is the first draft of an email, report, or speech our best effort. In fact, Anne Lamott in *Bird by Bird* argues that all authors should embrace the value of a "shitty first draft" on their way to the final work. Too often in B-school an assignment will have no shelf-life after it's submitted or delivered. Students get to the page or word limit and hit submit, or hit the time limit and stop talking. It's only through continual iteration that a product gets better.

At the GSB we devise ways for leaders to create a draft or do a rehearsal, get feedback, return to their work, and come back with another iteration. The easiest example of this is the LOWKeynote program, where students deliver "half of a TED talk." These nine-minute springtime talks are the result of a one-minute application video, a two-minute introduction on the first day of the program, a "first view" (often with notes in hand) in February and a "final view" with an audience of several hundred peers in March. These talks are remarkable because the design allows students to conceive, iterate, deliver, receive feedback, revise, and deliver again.

Feedback

Several times throughout a class term I will tell students, "I love giving you feedback, but hate giving you grades." It can easily take me up to an hour to fully evaluate and grade an eight-minute mid-term talk. I commit to providing rich feedback on every element of every talk they deliver. Often, at first, this looks like stream-of-consciousness notes. Then I go back in and synthesize my comments into coherent action steps. (Otherwise, "lack of punctuation on slide 7" carries equal weight with a comment like "no clear thesis or call to action.")

For the first several years I taught, I saw my feedback as "the final answer" on the quality of a student's work. I often had the students complete feedback forms for each other when they delivered talks, but I didn't invest much time or attention in reviewing these. Over time, however, I found that these peer feedback forms (if well designed) were informational treasures to support the speaker. I've now started providing "feedback on the feedback" both for the recipient and the writer. If I disagree with a comment, I will write in the margins, "That wasn't my experience." If I agree with a comment I will circle or highlight it so the speaker knows it has particular merit. Each time I return grades, I indicate who the "feedback stars" were on the assignment, so everybody knows that I read and reviewed the feedback forms as well as the assignment.

I've come to see that leaders learn "on both sides of the microscope." They learn by observing and commenting upon their peers, and they learn by being observed and getting this feedback.

Stakes

Finally, I've begun to see how leveraging social media tools to bring leaders' work to a wider audience heightens the stakes.

Since 2009, I've curated a library of student presentations on YouTube. These presentations represent final assignments in my course. The title of one of these talks, "Make Body Language Your Superpower," has over 3.5 million views. Knowing that students may be able to use coursework to expand their digital footprints adds a weight to the assignment beyond what I could offer on my own.

In 2012, we expanded this opportunity for GSB students by creating the LOWKeynotes program, which provides students an opportunity to craft a talk that is taped, posted on YouTube, and seen around the world.

And in 2014 I began publishing student blogs—first on WordPress, and later on Medium. The external pressure of a mass audience invites the students' focus in a way that no assignment "for the prof" could ever do. I'm delighted to see how many of my students use their public blogs or YouTube videos as examples of their talent on their own LinkedIn profiles. If done right, this aspect of their digital footprints carries more weight than an individual grade on a transcript.

So, on the foundation of individuality, relevance, iteration, feedback, and stakes we built a remarkable container for leaders to travel from uncertainty, to competence, to expertise, to mastery. You too can travel the same continuum using the lessons and activities this book provides. You cannot learn to swim by watching swim practice from the bleachers—you gotta get in the water. I hope you will dive in and get wet through the process. Don't just read this book . . . experience it!

Part 1 Speaking with Conviction and Writing for Impact

1 Adopting a Communication Mindset

Consider your communication mindset as a platform—every time you deliver a message, whether it's verbal or non-verbal, written or spoken, you'll stand on your communication mindset as the basis for all you do. Your communication mindset will ask you to think strategically, analytically, and empathetically about your audience and what matters to them. It will ask you to clarify the work that your communication is meant to do. And it will invite you to make choices about the words, channels, visuals, and multimedia assets that will comprise your message. It is not only a starting place, but the foundation for all effective communication. So let's dive in.

Know Your AIM

Nearly every class, workshop, or seminar I've led in the past decade at Stanford and beyond has begun with one simple yet elegant framework (Figure 1.1). So, of course, my first book should also begin in the same fashion. It's not just at the heart of all I teach and coach around communication, but I believe it's at the heart of all great leadership communication.

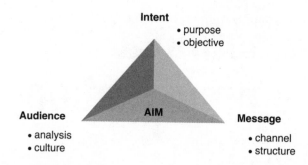

Figure 1.1 AIM triangle
Source: L. Russell and M. Munter, *Guide to Presentations*

While I wish I had developed it, there's nothing that I've seen or created on my own that's a better place for a leader to start. Lynn Russell (then at Columbia Business School) and Mary Munter (then at Dartmouth's Tuck School) co-created this model and included it in their book *Guide to Presentations*. But I believe it applies equally well to written and interpersonal communication as well as presentations. I've deployed this on ten-foot-high slides behind me at the Qualtrics Summit and sketched it on the back of a napkin at Starbucks while coaching an entrepreneur on her startup. It really does offer a beginning for most of the important communication that we engage in.

Order is important here . . . crucial, in fact. We must begin first in the shoes (or seats) of our audience. Once we know who we are addressing, we have to clarify our intent; what do we want them to do, think, or feel as a result of this communication? Only by clarifying Audience and Intent can we move on to Message. Inboxes around the planet are chock full of emails the recipient does not need to see, because too many people "blast out a message" rather than slowing down to tailor the communication to the right audience for the right reason (e.g., Intent).

Let's explore each of these elements in order. Let's begin with Audience.

Audience: The Starting Point for All Communication

I challenge leaders to devise as many methods of audience analysis as possible. "How can you get to know your readers before they open the email or pick up the pitch book? How can you learn about an audience before you are in front of them?" Typically, the responses I get fall into three broad categories: online research, personal contacts, and "creative espionage."

LinkedIn and Google searches top the online examples; finding information about individuals, groups, or firms with whom you plan to communicate has never been easier. It's relatively simple to find company bio pages, recent conference presentations, or public blog sites. Those who dig a little deeper may find their way to Glassdoor to research a firm or leader; this site often offers more subjective information, as its entries are largely provided by former employees—many of whom may have a bit of an ax to grind. Go deeper still, and you may find yourself amid 10-K reports on publicly traded firms, briefs on non-profits, and other forms of disclosure information that's public but not as quickly surfaced. In my reputation management class, we discuss the fact that almost everything online is permanent; once posted, even if taken down, it can still often be discovered.

Leveraging personal contacts makes up the second, often deeper, round of analysis. Can I find somebody in the audience to serve as a "mini focus group" for my message? Can I test out a few phrases or stories with a sample audience before I use them on my actual audience? Further, if I can find somebody who has recently spoken to this group who's willing to share that experience, all the better. The true gold is finding somebody who failed with this group and can share why. They might be able to tell you, "We were pitching a software solution, but they've shifted all their funding to cloud-based startups." Or: "I focused my recommendations on global expansion right when the firm announced layoffs and cost-cutting measures." While LinkedIn provides a great resource in and of itself, it can also yield valuable ideas about who you might contact for a one-on-one conversation. When I'm searching for a personal contact, I look both at who is currently at the firm, and who has recently left the firm or group. Recent employees may be able to be much more candid than current ones.

On that note, here's a tip about your "gatekeeper" when you first approach a new organization: mine your conversation with that person effectively. If someone at the firm is arranging your visit, pepper that person with questions at both a macro and micro level. Everything from "What has marked the success of recent speakers?" to "Do the men in your office wear jackets and ties to work?" is fair game. If you've been invited to submit a column or blog for a publication, likewise, ask them to share two or three examples of successful recent submissions.

Over the years I've enjoyed the strategies my MBA students have provided in the realm of "creative espionage." They have found social media posts on Instagram and Snapchat that mention the firm or individual. Some have gone so far as to apply for a job at a firm they wish to solicit for business to see how the firm represents itself to prospective employees. I've known people who've posed as secret shoppers and attended information sessions or participated in online webinars to better understand a firm and its offerings. One student (jokingly, I think!) shared the strategy of figuring out the "watering hole" for a team of interest to him and hanging out there to see what casual conversation he could overhear.

I often share the story of my colleague Ray McNulty, president of the National Dropout Prevention Network, who was invited to deliver a workshop on a Saturday morning for a group of public school teachers. This "mandatory in-service" was far from popular with the faculty who were required to attend. He arrived early and the host had not yet shown up to open the door. He listened intently as the teachers began to assemble, grousing about the need to come listen to this "expert" on a Saturday morning. They were a bit sheepish when they realized who he was when the person with the key arrived and welcomed him.

Let me be clear: I don't endorse duplicitous or deceptive measures for audience research; but I do appreciate the lengths that some leaders will go to better understand their audience before they try to write or speak to them. If only more leaders went to this effort.

It's also crucial to emphasize that any time we communicate with others, there is both a primary and secondary audience. Our primary audience is on the "to" line of the email or seated in front of us when we speak. These audience members are the primary reason for the communication to occur. Anybody with whom they choose to share the message would then be a secondary audience. Table 1.1 shows typical primary and secondary audiences with whom a leader may communicate.

Table 1.1 Primary and Secondary Audiences

Primary Audience Members	Secondary Audience Members
Regional directors	The field managers they supervise
Junior partners at a VC firm	Senior partners who will decide to invest
A journalist	All of those who read her column
Advisors to a senior leader	The senior leader
Sales team members	Customers who will ultimately buy

Thus far our discussion of audience members has been around intentional primary audiences: individuals or groups of people whom we've designated to receive our communication. Yet we cannot end this section without a discussion of unintended secondary audiences. An email we intend "for your eyes only" is forwarded to a wider group. A person who was listed as BCC mistakenly hits "reply all" and comes "out of hiding." A disgruntled employee or customer secretly films an interaction with you and posts it on YouTube for the world to see. The classic example I provide is Mitt Romney's 2012 election bid, when he thought he was having a private conversation with a limited group of high-net-worth donors. But unbeknownst to Romney, a bartender with an iPhone propped against a water pitcher recorded and then broadcast the entire chat widely, arming the Obama campaign with controversial sound bites for the remaining six weeks of the campaign. As a leader, you need not cower from such communication possibilities, but should simply commit to owning your communication so that if an unintended audience hears or reads it, your words still do the work you intend them to do.

Audience-centric communication provides the foundation for everything else in this book. It's not simply the first part of the AIM model, it's the place all leaders must begin their work to inform, influence, or inspire others. Occasionally a student will ask me for a letter of recommendation without telling me the name of the recipient. I say I'm willing to write the letter, but that it's going to be much stronger and more effective if I can tailor it to the organization and role to which the student is applying. Without a clear audience in mind, how can a leader provide an impactful message?

Intent: Your Reason for Communication

Now we move to Intent, the second part of the Munter/Russell model. Certainly there are numerous ways to describe the goal, objective, or outcome of a communication. I like their choice of "Intent" not simply because of the great acronym it creates, but because of the clarity of the word. It's both the intention in my mind as a speaker or writer, and the action in the minds of the audience. It's not simply what I want the audience to think, say, or do, it's what they choose to do as a result of the communication.

Take the example of a senior Stanford hospital leader—we'll call him Ken, although that's not really his name. I was coaching Ken to lead a town hall meeting with his staff. Halfway through a rehearsal of his presentation, I interrupted and said, "What's your intent?"

He replied as many of us might: "I want to impress them."

"Okay, great, Ken," I said. "But that's all about you! What do you want the staff to think, say, or do as a result of this town hall?"

After a short pause, he said, "Oh, I see. . . . I want them to be impressed."

"Fair enough!" I said. "But that's still all about you. What do you want them to do?"

He paused and then said, "Treat patients with dignity."

The room (and the talk) shifted in that insight. We did not have to make sweeping changes, but now we had a north star to which we could align our efforts. Without clarity of intent, we are like a ship without a compass. We might somehow show up at our location, but it's not by design.

In March 2019 I shared the stage at the annual Qualtrics X4 Summit with Barack Obama and Oprah Winfrey. (I'm pretty sure Barack and Oprah don't mention me if they describe the occasion; there were hundreds of presenters. But my talk on Storytelling with Data was indeed between their two keynotes. I'll take it!) I was incredibly moved by Oprah and her clarity of intention. She shared that she made a choice very early in her career to not produce a single episode of her show without a clear statement of intent with which everybody on the production team could align. She told the audience that the event that triggered this clarity was an episode she produced about infidelity. On this episode, a male guest, seated between his wife and his mistress, shared that he'd gotten his mistress pregnant. Oprah acknowledged, "No wife should endure that on national television. And I had to ask myself and my team, 'What's our intent here?'" She went on to share, in her signature empowering style, that when we align our actions with our intent great things come to pass. We're better able to cause our communication to make an impact we intend, and more importantly, an impact in which we can believe.

Back on earth with us mortals, I urge my students to set a single clear intent for every communication they have—something from the audience's viewpoint that the speaker intends to bring forward. Here are some examples:

- Embrace our company's technology
- Endorse my candidacy publicly
- Invite me to their office for a longer conversation
- Agree to take on a volunteer commitment to lead this effort
- Eliminate negative references to a former employee

Whether we are designing and creating a web page, delivering a TED talk, proposing marriage to our spouse, or sending a tweet about an upcoming theater production, we need to be crystal clear on our intent before we open our mouths or hit send on our keyboards.

How Communication Intent Has Evolved in Silicon Valley

One of the many colleagues I've come to know at Stanford is Raymond Nasr, a lecturer who specializes in communication. He offers his insights within a popular elective, Entrepreneurship and Venture Capital, which is taught by Eric Schmidt and Peter Wendell. Raymond served as Eric's communication director and speechwriter for decades at Novell and later at Google.

Raymond recalls that in the 1970s and 1980s, communication was largely a "secretarial function," and certainly not strategic. "In the late 1970s and early 1980s, communications as a profession was not what it is today by any stretch of the imagination. It was on the margin. A notch above secretarial,

(Continued)

largely administrative—and it really was often a case of an administrative assistant or a secretary taking down notes from a CEO, putting it into a format that would be distributable on paper, and giving it to the members of the press. They would in turn write the story about what the CEO wanted to say. So managing the narrative was dead easy. It would be a press release with the quotes embedded into the *San Jose Mercury* news article, and that was it.

"But then there was this company called Apple. Their strategic communication was revolutionary. They realized that there was so much power in narrative that they needed to manage every element of it, in-house. See, before, often the chip guys and the hardware guys would hire a PR firm to take that notepaper from the secretary, turn it into a press release, and put it on some fancy letterhead. The PR firms had relationships with the press corps. So companies would hire an agency to do PR work. Instead, Apple said no, we're going to manage every element of our complete experience. From the launch of the products, to the events, the financial industry analysts, product publicity, and packaging to executive communication—everything is going to be integrated under one umbrella."

Raymond sees this evolution as both key to his success at the biggest names in tech (Apple, Novell, and Google) but also as a key ingredient to our success at Stanford. Our community already had the appetite for skills in strong and strategic communication, so we began to provide valuable courses that met this need. The fact that icons Wendell and Schmidt purposefully embed Raymond Nasr into their course speaks volumes about how valued communication is as a discipline within the Silicon Valley ethos, and why it has grown so steadily at Stanford.

Message: Delivering on Your Intent with Words That Matter

We might say that the final element of the Munter/Russell model is where the magic happens. Once you've familiarized yourself with your audience and clarified your intent, you're ready to communicate. You're ready to share your message.

If audience is the "who" and intent is the "why," message is the "how." So now the question I urge students to answer is how they will structure and channel their message.

The channel for your message is the medium you choose for your communication. If you need to scale your communication to a broad audience, maybe you'll choose to prepare a talk that can be filmed and shared on YouTube; or you might choose to write a blog post that you can publish broadly, such as on Medium or LinkedIn. Consider what medium will be most approachable for your audience: earning your colleague's buy-in right before the big meeting might be a job for a Slack message or a chat in the hallway, whereas a thank-you note for a job interview might be best accomplished through a handwritten note (what can I say: I'm old-fashioned). Some questions to ask yourself before you make this choice: How far do I need my message to go? How long do I want my message to "last"? How formal is my message? What medium is easiest for my audience to access, use, or understand?

Too often we rely on just a few familiar channels instead of considering the wide range of choices we have to deliver our message. One activity I often do with my MBA students is to co-create a list on the board of all the possible channels available to share a message. I draw three long lines across the whiteboard making a row for Oral, Blended, and Written. Across the top I write "highly interactive" in the top left corner, "moderately interactive" in the center, and "minimally interactive" on the right corner. Then, for the next 15 to 20 minutes, we come up with different channels available to share a message: send an email, call a meeting, write a memo, tweet, send a text, deliver a talk. For each medium a student mentions, we discuss how interactive this choice would be. Often that has to do with how many recipients there are for the communication; a meeting with just one other person is highly interactive, but if 1,000 people are in the room not so much. Once enough stickies have made it to the whiteboard, students begin to see the wide array of choices available to them. Leaders committed to inspiring action on the part of their audience may have to be creative in what vehicle they choose to share that message. Further, a complex message may require multiple channels to achieve the desired result. I may need to send a teaser email in advance, deliver a great presentation, follow up with two or three key stakeholders, and send a final email synthesizing the message and reminding people of the action needed.

Figure 1.2 shows an example of just a few.

	Highly Interactive	Moderately Interactive	Minimally Interactive
Oral	1 on 1 Conversation Phone Call	Small Group Meeting	Voicemail Town Hall Podcast
Blended	Video Call	Meeting with Slides Live Webinar	Posted Recording of Webinar
Written	Text Slack Shared Document	Email Facebook Post Blast email	Handwritten Note Snail Mail Printed Bound Document

Figure 1.2 Communication channel choices by interaction level

Yet, we fall back all too often on the two most familiar methods: calling a meeting or writing an email. When students begin to look at this more robust menu of options, they begin to see how becoming a more strategic communicator is possible. It becomes easy to see that a more complex message may require a mix of several different channels, strategically designed in concert with one another.

Once you've chosen your channel, it's time to get down to the business of structuring your message. Many of my students choose to use an outline to generate some structure. What are the main points you wish to make in your communication? What are the key reasons and examples you can offer in support of those points? Once you've assembled a robust scaffold for your communication, you're ready to write, speak, chat, text, parlay, meet, or communicate in whatever other channel you've selected. Let your information about your audience inform your tone and word choice. (Don't worry, we'll talk about this process in depth in our upcoming chapters on speaking and writing.)

Starting with AIM sets you up to speak to the exact audience before you for the reasons that matter to you. This useful pre-work need not be time-consuming or laborious, but those few minutes you devote to investigating your audience, intent, and message will pay dividends when it's time to share your thoughts with the world and inspire others to action.

Beyond AIM: The Leadership Communication Canvas

If you have a complex message that needs to be delivered in a high-stakes setting, you might expand upon AIM by taking a more nuanced style of preparation. The model we have found helpful is a nine-box Leadership Communication Canvas, which encourages you to take a thoughtful, multifaceted approach to sharing your content.

At a business school like Stanford it's not unexpected that we would be a veritable factory of communication. While we witness (and often coach) an enormous volume of material, until 2007 there was not a standard approach to help students create communication they wished to share. MBAs come into our program with strong—dare I say excellent—experience in writing and speaking through their undergraduate degrees and their work as bankers, consultants, managers, and entrepreneurs. But we had as many approaches to creating communication as we had enrolled students. The solution we found was to guide students—with the help of a professional communication coach—to look not at "templates to complete" for documents and presentations, but rather a "canvas to create" whenever facing an issue that requires a thoughtful communication strategy.

Many of our students are extremely familiar with Alexander Osterwalder and Yves Pigneur's business model canvas from their best-selling book *Business Model Generation*. This widely adopted, open-source approach to creating and launching a business provides the necessary framing and questions for any entrepreneur. The authors describe the business model canvas as "a shared language for describing, visualizing, assessing, and changing business models" (12). It's been adapted for use in non-profit ventures, government initiatives, and internal campaigns within larger firms. Its simplicity and focus have made it an essential part of many entrepreneurs' (and entrepreneurship faculty members') toolkits.

Since this was a language many of our students already knew, we adapted their work with a specific focus on the needs of a leader with a powerful message to share. We've provided the canvas here for you to see (Figure 1.3), and blank copies can be downloaded at http://www.jdschramm.com/mastery for you to use in creating content for your next communication. The nine boxes provide categories for the key aspects of any communication (written, spoken, or both). While we will treat the boxes sequentially, the art of crafting a key communication must be more fluid and organic. Begin anywhere on the canvas you wish—in fact, change the size and shape of the boxes to suit the needs of your particular mission. As you know from our discussion of AIM, however, we will begin on the far right side with Audience.

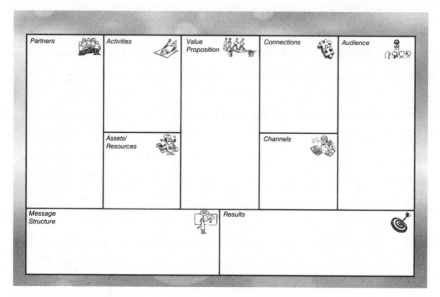

Figure 1.3 Leadership communication canvas

Audience: Who Needs to Hear (or Read) Your Message?

Yes, welcome back: we're right back at AIM. By now, you already know that all effective leadership communication begins with a focus on the recipient. The first step a leader must take is to define who precisely needs to hear the message being created. This may seem obvious in some cases. For example, "I want prospective employees to hear my message and join my firm." But for a leader communicating in a complex and nuanced way, it's crucial to ponder carefully not just who I *can* reach . . . but who I *must* reach. It is not simply the people seated in front of me (or on the "to" line of an email). This may be my primary audience, but in all leadership communication there is a secondary audience. A pitch to a junior partner at a VC firm will only be funded when a senior partner endorses it and takes it to an investment committee. A cover letter in application for a job may be reviewed by an HR recruiter who decides whether or not the hiring manager will ever see or know of this candidate. At this phase of a communicator's work, it is crucial to brainstorm all the possible primary and secondary audience members, then settle on a short list of the most crucial audience members to target. It's ideal if somewhere along the way a leader can pull a "test audience" together to read or view a communication and respond before it goes forward. The greater the stakes of the message, the more useful a test audience can be for a leader's success.

Value Proposition: What Do You Bring to the Table for This Message?

Staring back from the center of the canvas is the question, "Why you?" Why are you the one to bring forth this communication? What is your credibility, your source that powers you to make this message come forward? In large organizations there may be some debate over whose signature should be at the bottom of a communication; in campaigns much thought goes into whether a candidate or a representative should deliver a message. As a leader with a communication to share, what is your authority to speak or write on the subject? If there is a gap in your knowledge or people's perception of you, can that be offset before you deliver a message? Or if not, can the message be crafted in such a way that the gap is not an impediment to your success?

Channels: What Vehicle Will You Use to Share Your Message?

At times your channel will already be chosen for you. If your boss calls a meeting and asks you to provide an update on a deal you are trying to close, the vehicle is an in-person meeting with your colleagues. If you receive an email from a colleague requesting your input on an idea, you hit reply and, voilá, you have chosen the channel of email to share your message. But for high-stakes messages, it is important to brainstorm all of the possible channels available to deliver a message. Feel free to review the exercise in Figure 1.2 we share in the AIM section of this book for more on how to brainstorm a rich canvas of channels for your communication.

Connections: What Will Engage the Audience?

Earlier we considered how to get the right bodies in the room (or right eyes on our report). Now that we've made that decision, how do we engage the audience with our topic? A writer can do this with a compelling, clear subject line—one that is directly tied to an action item and engages the reader to open the email. Speakers can use storytelling, statistics, or questions to bring the audience into their world. But once you get the audience there, you must embrace them to remain engaged. Much has been written and shared about effective storytelling skills for leaders. (See my personal favorite books on this in appendix D.) In fact I'm stunned that the topic is, hands down, the greatest request I get from prospective consulting clients. People are moved by a well-told story and seek out the ability to craft effective stories when they write and speak. When leaders entertain questions, they often experience the greatest level of engagement of the entire presentation; in fact, many leaders have found that they continually reduce the time spent "telling the troops a message" and more time "fielding questions." It is in this moment of personal sharing that we can create the greatest connection.

Assets/Resources: What Do You Already Have or Can You Develop to Move Your Audience?

Many times a great talk or blog begins with a story, a photo, an experience, a statistic, an insight. Consider the building blocks you already have for a communication. Use whatever form is comfortable for you to capture these ideas into a single place. Much to my husband's chagrin, my favorite collection spot is a large sheet of sticky top-flip chart paper. My study is often covered with these sheets as a way to visually capture the elements of my next HBR blog or keynote presentation. Others work with a sketch pad and illustrations, like Dan Roam suggests in *The Back of the Napkin*. Still others prefer a spreadsheet or document on their tablet or laptop. Where you pile up your inventory of assets doesn't matter; what matters is that you pile them up. Consider TED talks, cartoons, photographs, charts, graphs, anecdotes—anything that could be fashioned into the communication you are creating. For students doing a traditional report or essay, these may be the "note cards of evidence" that can be arranged and rearranged into a clear and compelling argument. (Yes, I realize I may be dating myself by referencing note cards!) Often it's useful to dream about what resources you wish you had. "Find inspiring story of faculty interaction on a global study trip" can be a placeholder for research I need to complete in order to finish my communication.

While it's certainly true that in brainstorming, no idea is a bad idea, to be efficient you will want to consider how much effort you'll need to acquire your assets. A leader needs to discern what level of investment is warranted for this level of return. In the TED library you'll find countless examples of talks that used vivid assets to help the speaker deliver a message: Jill Bolte holding a human brain, Bill Gates opening a jar of mosquitoes, Jamie Oliver emptying a wheelbarrow full of sugar on stage, or Lior Zoraf asking the audience to crowdsource the weight of a live ox next to him on the stage. Make it happen if the investment of obtaining it will be worth the reward.

Activities: How Can You Reach the Audience That Needs to Hear Your Message?

These actions all exist in the preparation portion to be sure your well-crafted communication doesn't fall on the proverbial "deaf ears."

What do you do to ensure the right people get into the room to hear what you have to say? Who can you get to "invite" people to your meeting or forward your email with a note of their own endorsement? An example of how publishing used to function may be helpful here to illustrate what NOT to do. Authors often work in solitude creating a book. When done they turn it over to a team of editors who finish the work and prepare it to be printed. Finally, a different team of publicists steps in to schedule book signings and events once the book is finished. Many an author has painfully pulled up in front of a bookstore to see a timid and small crowd to buy a handful of the books. This activity was not reaching the right people (or anybody really). What activities can you take on while creating your communication to ensure people will show up to the meeting, read the blog, or attend the event? Leaders today must cause the audience more than ever before.

Partners: Who Can Help You Do This?

Another program at Stanford, the Arbuckle Leadership Fellows, explains in their promotional materials that you are a leader because others follow. If they don't follow, then you are not leading. This is abundantly clear in communication. To be truly effective you will need to rely on others to help you create, test, refine, and disseminate the message. While crafting a message, consider (and capture in a list) those whose partnership will be crucial to the success you seek. Tactically you may need a designer to assist with slides, an editor to clean up your report, or a coach to rehearse content with you. Strategically you may need to get some early adopters who agree with your message to get an advance copy of a blog or a preview of what you will share at a management team meeting. Perhaps the message you are sharing will be supported if you have an executive champion within the organization or a thought leader outside the organization who can echo and amplify what you write or speak. Know who these individuals are and how to approach them so you're successful at delivering your message.

In one of the programs I founded at Stanford, LOWKeynotes, I encourage students at this stage of development to list people they do not yet know who they want to enroll as partners in getting their talks created and delivered. I challenge them to find the academics on campus who have published in this field, the leaders of organizations committed to similar ideals, or the luminaries who have already spoken or written about this topic and seek their help. It is never easier to reach out to thought leader than when you are a student and can ask their help in a project you are creating. But readers who are not students can still approach others for input. Use LinkedIn, for example, to see how closely connected you may be to just the right partner for your message. Finally, don't ignore the value of devil's advocates in helping you create your message. It is invaluable to have a critic who is not afraid to poke holes in your report or find flaws in your presentation structure. Doris Kearns Goodwin's remarkable book *Team of Rivals* paints a compelling portrait of how President Lincoln sought out this resource. Barack Obama employed a similar approach by asking two of his most vociferous adversaries in the primary (Joe Biden and Hillary Clinton) to play key roles in his administration. Who can you engage to be your rigorous critic as you develop your message?

Message Structure: How Will You Frame the Message?

Now armed with all the ammunition from the top seven boxes, it is time to assemble your structure. The genre you've chosen (op/ed piece, for example) may dictate a bit of a structure to you. Or you may have a completely blank canvas (pun intended) as you decide how to begin, develop, and close your message. At a fundamental level the advice passed on from preachers since the early 1900s remains sound: Tell 'em what you're gonna say, tell 'em, and tell 'em what you just told them. Most solid communications have an introduction that previews, a body that delivers content in a clear way, and a conclusion that reviews and calls the audience to some level of action. That tried-and-true approach may work just fine for a simple email or a short, informative portion of a meeting. However, a more nuanced structure may be needed for a new product pitch to investors or a TED-style talk as a keynote.

The research and writings of Nancy Duarte provide me inspiration when I am creating a talk. Through her work designing hundreds of thousands of presentations over the years at her firm, Duarte Design, Nancy has uncovered a simple sparkline that underlies all great presentations (Figure 1.4).

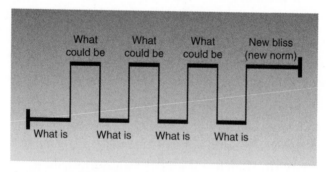

Figure 1.4 Nancy Duarte's "Sparkline" for great presentations
Source: From *Resonate by* Nancy Duarte, Wiley 2010.

A speaker must begin with a sense of the status quo—"what is"—and then articulate "what could be." A strong persuasive presentation will tack back and forth, like a sailor against the winds of resistance, between what is and what could be until, near the end, the speaker calls the audience to a "new bliss" and engages them with a clear call to action. In her book *Resonate*, Duarte details how this sparkline can be found in talks as disparate as Martin Luther King Jr.'s "I Have a Dream" speech, Eva Peron's appeal to the people of Argentina from the balcony, and Steve Jobs's introduction of the new iPhone. As you create the structure of your communication, consider the contrast between what currently exists and what is possible. Outlining these distinctions as you deliver can bring the audience along with you.

(*Side note:* I strongly encourage you to purchase and devour Nancy Duarte's book *Resonate*, but if you cannot imagine reading another book right now, take 20 minutes and watch her great TEDx East talk, "The Secret Structure of Great Talks." This quick view will offer you the key aspects of the sparkline in Nancy's own words. The iTunes version of her book includes video and audio files to the great talks she analyzes. I personally reference both the digital and print versions regularly.)

Results: What Do You Want the Audience to Think, Say, or Do After You Communicate?

Many leaders will begin their message development in this bottom right quadrant with a clear statement of intent. Occasionally a leader may have a multilayered intent—for example, "Today I want them to visit my website and contribute, but ultimately I am committed to ending the scourge of slavery on the planet." Jim Collins's great work on BHAGs (Big Hairy Audacious Goals) has inspired thousands to dream big and capture in writing what you wish to achieve. We only can achieve a BHAG by writing and speaking about our intended results with others. In an academic environment, I get stymied by students who tell me that the result they want is to "get an A on the paper." Grades on assignments are such a small goal. Instead, write to change lives, organizations, and the world. Write to cause a business leader to adopt your strategy; write to not simply summarize what the case provided, but to synthesize that information into clear insights, and you will earn the A. Set your eyes on a result that you believe is attainable, but have your wider vision on the greater difference you can make.

The Leadership Communication canvas is not the framework I deploy for every talk I coach or deliver. But when the stakes are high and when the message has the potential to last, then I do turn to this canvas. Kara and I even created a canvas for this book, which you can see on my website at jdschramm.com/mastery. When the going gets tough, knowing that this clear plan can guide you is a crucial form of motivation.

2 Speaking with Conviction

When it comes to speaking with conviction, the good news is that we're all starting at an advantage. Every one of us has spoken successfully, meaningfully, and authentically before, and every one of us has—at one time or another—felt fully convicted of our ideas and convinced others to feel the same. The magic happens when we can investigate this process enough that we're able to repeat it consistently and, particularly, in high-stakes moments.

But while speaking may seem like a monolithic practice, it's actually made up of some important component parts. Before we can begin to speak, we need to manage our anxiety about speaking so that we can do our best—and feel comfortable in the process. And once we open our mouths, we're actually communicating in three important ways:

- Verbal (what we say)
- Vocal (how we say it)
- Visual (what they see)

Think of anxiety management and VVV working like the different parts of an orchestra. You'll still make beautiful music when only one of these elements is excelling, but approaching mastery of all of them together creates the kind of harmony that makes for truly compelling communication.

Managing Your Anxiety

Ask leaders whether they have anxiety about speaking, presenting, or leading a meeting, and you'll get any number of answers—everything from, "I don't get anxious—I've got this!" to "Depends who's in the room," to "I'm absolutely terrified." Regardless of our personal attitudes toward anxiety, we all find ourselves experiencing it from time to time when the stakes are high. As you're preparing to lead at your best, set yourself up for success by thinking about anxiety as a tool that you can manage: as an asset, not a liability.

I usually think of three primary resources when I approach the issue of managing anxiety: our GSB colleague Matt Abrahams; organizational psychologist Adam Grant; and social psychologist Amy Cuddy.

The most hands-on but possibly least-known is Matt Abrahams's book *Speaking Up Without Freaking Out*. I require all my students to read this short directory of proven strategies to reduce anxiety. A team of my students adapted his book into a short YouTube lesson, entitled "Embrace Your Freaking Out," which provides a brief and engaging synthesis of some of Abrahams's techniques. At this printing it has nearly 10,000 views on YouTube and is steadily rising. Among many other fine ideas in this book, Matt encourages leaders to reframe speaking as a conversation rather than as a presentation. By recasting a performance as a collaborative event, communication can feel more like a chat and less like a confrontation—something to win or lose. Whereas there may be one "right way" to deliver a performance, there are many ways to conduct a conversation. Take the pressure off of yourself by using conversational language, asking questions of your audience to engage them in dialogue, and mentally reframing the event as a conversation.

Another reframe that I really like is moving from the mind-set "I'm anxious" to the mindset "I'm excited." It seems like such a simple little tip, but as Adam Grant discusses in his book *Originals*, it's a game-changer for leaders to reframe presentations, meetings, and conversations as opportunities rather than threats. This is the moment when you can make your anxiety work for you as a tool, a propulsive force rather than a block to action. I ask leaders in my classes to read the relevant excerpt on this theme from Adam's book, and we then work on exercises to get used to the feeling of saying "I'm excited" even when we feel anxious. My co-teachers in Strategic Communication and I lead our students through an entire session on anxiety management early in the course each quarter. We first try to normalize the experience of anxiety. It's not an unfamiliar feeling, and in fact, the adrenaline can help to ensure that your passion comes through. Our GSB colleague Burt Alper loves to remind students that the physical symptoms of anxiety (sweaty palms and racing heart, for example) are legacy signs of an oncoming attack. Yet never in his career, no matter how poorly he's performed while speaking, has a lion ever attacked him during a presentation. This mantra—"Where's the lion?"—becomes shorthand for our students to embrace the situation, but not let it overwhelm them.

Chances are, when you think of managing your anxiety, the phrase "power poses" comes to mind. Amy Cuddy's TED talk and subsequent book, *Presence*, detail her fascinating research into the connection between our minds and our bodies to manage anxiety. The power poses she describes in these resources have been popularized worldwide, and for good reason. Cuddy establishes that we feel powerful when we expand our bodies; when we take up more space, we immediately feel more confident. In fact, doing so has been shown to lower cortisol, the stress hormone, by as much as 25 percent.

So not only do we feel more powerful emotionally, but our bodies require less compensation to deal with the stress of leading.

To be sure, there are academic researchers who question the validity of Cuddy's work. In fact, one of her coauthors, Dana Carney at Berkeley, has distanced herself from the research. Those who want to dive into the granular value of P-values and sample size can find interesting debates online. But I know that for me and my students, power poses work. Even if using a pose is the proverbial Dumbo's feather, students who practice and use a power pose before a key meeting, interview, or presentation show up with greater confidence.

Take an example from my own experience: Shortly after I learned of this tactic, I found myself sitting in the lobby of Bentall Kennedy, a major real estate investment firm. I was waiting to go into the conference room and pitch my services as a presentation skills coach for their senior management team. But instead of reaching for my phone and handling a few more emails as I might usually do, I put my phone on airplane mode, placed it back in my pocket, picked up the *Wall Street Journal* from the coffee table, and sat in the lobby reading. For me, the most vivid visual of the difference between a low-power position and a high-power position is the comparison between opening a newspaper with arms outstretched, and being hunched over an iPhone typing emails with one's thumbs. That particular morning, I consciously chose to expand rather than to shrink. I chose the newspaper over the iPhone, and walked into the meeting clear and confident—and I walked out successful, with the gig. I continue to share Amy Cuddy's 2012 TED talk and expect my students to at least try striking a power pose to see if this strategy can work for them to reduce anxiety and build confidence.

If you didn't have any anxiety about speaking, you wouldn't be human (or maybe you'd just be a very seasoned speaker!). Anxiety can be a gift that increases your energy and motivates you to speak from a place of excitement. But where it's not serving your message, remember that you have the keys to open this gateway between nervous communication and comfortable communication.

Verbal, Vocal, Visual: Your Recipe for Successful Communication

Before we get into the nuts and bolts of how each element of "verbal, vocal, visual" works, let's consider the way all three work together. The verbal element is the actual words you say; if we placed a stenographer in the back of the room while you were presenting, their transcript would reflect the verbal element of your communication. The vocal element is how you use the instrument of your voice: your intonation, your volume, your pace, and your inflection. Finally, the visual element reflects your non-verbal communication: your gestures, your facial expression, your body language, and your personal appearance.

When you think about these three elements of oral communication—verbal, vocal, and visual—which do you consider to have the most amount of power over an audience? For years, I introduced this section of my teaching with Albert Mehrabian's research about the correlation between the verbal, vocal, and visual aspects of a presentation. When I began my teaching career, I inherited slides that vividly showed that only 7 percent of our impact on an audience is made by the actual words that we share, the verbal; that vocal communication—how we say it—holds 38 percent of our power over an audience; and that fully 55 percent of our influence over an audience is communicated through the visual—what the audience sees. His outdated research, performed in 1967 and published in 1974, has been used by public speaking instructors and authors for decades (okay, basically my entire life) to show that 93 percent of what we communicate is non-verbal. Scores of books on the shelves in my office cite his research, incorrectly, as do many of my colleagues in the profession. People I trust greatly, from Nick Morgan, former editor of the Harvard Communication Letter, to Chris Anderson, the CEO of TED, have publicly debunked this misinterpretation of Mehrabian's research. Apparently even Dr. Mehrabian, now nearing 80, requested that public speaking coaches stop misusing his research. Yet, like an urban legend, the "Mehrabian Myth" persists.

So, while I don't believe audiences will understand fully 93 percent of our message without our words, I do like to introduce his name and research, admit that it's not that black and white, but emphasize that our body language provides a great deal more influence than we would expect. What I most appreciate from his work is the clear (and alliterative) distinction of the three elements that occur within all sorts of communication. His work in interpersonal communication does strongly signal that when there is disagreement between what people say and what their body language indicates, we rely more on body language than spoken language.

Verbal: What You Say

What we say: this is what most of us think of first when we're crafting a message. These are the words we use to make our ideas known. From the very first words we choose, we begin to indicate a level of formality (or informality) by how we describe our ideas. The way we use language can add to our credibility; on the flip side, if we use too much jargon that our audience doesn't understand, we can harm our credibility—or at the very least make it difficult for our audience to understand our ideas.

Consider for a moment some of the products we rely on every day that began as little-known startup innovations. What we now know as FedEx once came with an informative tagline: "Federal Express: When it absolutely, positively has to get there overnight." Or consider ZipCars, with their tagline "Wheels when you want 'em." With these words, we get a quick sense of what these companies offer. The way we use language to describe our innovation can add to our credibility and engagement, or detract from it. Most of all, we want to be clear, and we want to be simple.

Ironically it may take quite a bit of time to craft a concise, clear message that conveys our ideas authentically and persuasively—but it is so worth the effort. The more care a leader spends crafting and editing a message to make it clear, the easier it will be for the audience to understand and act upon the message. As you prepare your communication, be intentional about the first words you're going to say. Will you begin with the problem you're solving? The solution you're offering? How will you open to capture (and keep!) your audience's attention? Then, be equally intentional about the final words you'll speak. What are the last words you'll leave with the audience to make them act, think, or feel differently? And finally, how will you transition between the different sections of your presentation so that there's a sense of cohesion?

Our words capture the audience's attention, highlight the key information they need to know, speak to their biases and concerns, and leave them with some thoughts that will propel them to action. Think of them as the fabric from which your presentation is created. Fabric alone doesn't make a shirt—but you can't have a shirt without it.

Vocal: How You Say It

Your message can be beautifully structured, compellingly outlined, and strongly supported, but even the best planners among us can be undermined by something as simple as the sound of our own voices. When we deliver our ideas in a way that makes us seem unsure or detracts from the immediacy of our message, not only do we make it difficult for others to understand us, but we undermine our credibility. I urge my student leaders to be intentional about how they use the instrument of their voices—how loud, how soft, how quickly they speak to create excitement, and how slowly they speak for impact.

Without a doubt, the best way to assess your own vocal communication is to record yourself speaking. It's easy to make a quick audio or video recording of yourself on a smartphone or a computer. Try speaking about your ideas, your goals, your company, your projects, or your challenges. Then evaluate your vocal success against five important metrics:

- Pace
- Volume
- Clarity
- Filler words
- Animation

How's your pace? Are you speaking so quickly that we can't understand what you're trying to say? Or are you speaking so slowly that we're waiting in agony for your message to conclude? Vary your pace a little bit. Faster speeds can create energy in your presentation. Slowing down can add impact to an important point or make a certain statistic or story more memorable.

Think of your ideal volume not as being loud for loudness's sake—but as projecting your voice well enough that the back of the room can hear you clearly. You'll need to use a different level of projection in a room built for 30 people than in a room built for three. If you have a microphone on, you should be thoughtful about how you use your personal amplification in concert with the added amplification provided by the A/V system. Projection is really all about how we breathe. We're able to project most effectively when we breathe from our diaphragms. You can think of this action as breathing from the lower part of your stomach. It takes some work to strengthen this skill—and you can do so on your own or with a speech coach—but doing so will allow you to project more effectively, and it will give you the strength to deliver a longer presentation.

Clarity is a function of the words you choose and how you pronounce them. I want to be very careful about defining pronunciation here. I've been fortunate to work with many talented entrepreneurs who present and converse in a language that is not their primary language; many of them have accents that make their pronunciation different from those of a native speaker of that language. I don't believe you should ever try to eliminate your accent—in fact, your accent is part of what contributes to your credibility and informs the power you have as a speaker of multiple languages. But if there are words you speak that your audience has trouble understanding, you may need to do some special work on those particular words or phrases. Maybe there's another word you could use that is easier for you to pronounce. Or perhaps the solution may be to slow down and say those words twice. You could even consider putting those phrases on a screen behind you so that you're sure your audience understands the words you're using. Chapter Six begins with a discussion of the unique gifts and challenges a non-native speaker experiences when delivering a talk in English.

So far in this conversation about vocal communication, we've discussed the ways you present the words you've chosen to share in your message. But invariably, there will be moments that show up in your presentation that were never in your script. These are typically filler words or non-words that get in the way. A filler word might be "um," "uh," "like," "er," but it can also be any other word that doesn't add meaning to your sentence. Those might be words or phrases like "actually," "generally," or "to tell you the truth." It's kind of like the square in Scrabble that has no letter or points on it: it fills the space, but it doesn't move the conversation forward.

This can be a very difficult habit to break. Here's a strategy: First, as I mentioned earlier, it's invaluable to get an audio or video recording of yourself so you can increase your awareness of when and how filler words are sneaking in. Over time, you'll notice a pattern starting to emerge. Maybe you say "um" each time you look back at your slides. Maybe you begin your statements with a filler word, or offer filler words at transition points. First, focus on where these words show up. Then, focus on trying to reduce them. In a later section on non-native speakers, we cover several more elements of this aspect of communication, including an activity my coauthor Kara Levy designed on slowing down speech to ensure clarity.

Ultimately, you want to have a vocal quality with some animation. You'll want to be able to inject some life and energy into your presentation, but also to reach the lower registers of gravitas in the moments that require it. As we begin to look at vocal quality, there's a process that most speakers go through to break the bad habits that lead to unclear language, filler words, and lack of variety.

I've seen several illustrations of Maslow's four stages of learning over the years, but most like how Dom Moorhouse chose to illustrate them in Figure 2.1. We start from a place of unconscious incompetence. (Don't feel bad, it sounds much worse than it is.) Unconscious incompetence means that we're doing it wrong, and we aren't even aware that we're doing it wrong. This is when you add five "um"s to your sentence and you don't even hear yourself doing it. But don't worry; once you start working on your vocal quality, you won't be here for long.

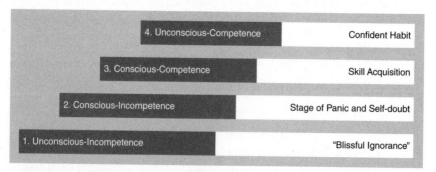

Figure 2.1 Maslow's stages of learning

Source: https://methodgrid.com/blog/10-building-a-firm-wide-sales-capability/

Once you're aware of your bad habits, you move to the next phase of the process: conscious incompetence. Now you're still making those same errors, but you're aware of them. As they say in the rooms of Alcoholics Anonymous, the first step is admitting you have a problem. You begin to hear that vocal tic where you say "as a matter of fact" every time you introduce an interesting data point. You start to become aware of the uptick at the end of your sentences. Progress!

Third, we move to a level of conscious competence. At this stage, you're aware of your habits and you're trying to correct them, but doing so requires a lot of focused attention. Speakers in this phase of conscious competence may speak in a voice that's a bit more stilted or stiff than they would like. They may deliver their material more slowly and demonstrate a great deal of focus on not including filler words. But it's that focused attention that will allow these speakers to get to the final stage of the process: unconscious competence.

This fourth and final phase of unconscious competence is the sweet spot where we don't even have to think about our vocal quality. Your better habits reveal themselves naturally, without requiring focused attention from you. I compare unconscious competence to a figure skater sailing around the ice, performing spins and jumps that look incredibly easy. But anyone watching knows that the skater has invested years of practice, iteration, and repetition to reach that level of unconscious competence. I often find that our students here at Stanford will spend a lot of time between the second and third stages, conscious incompetence and conscious competence. They become aware of their bad habits and begin focusing on reducing them, but as they begin to get more comfortable with one skill, another challenge will emerge to slip them back into conscious incompetence. They'll move back and forth between these two levels for some time until their commitment to practice takes them to that fourth level. When we reach unconscious competence, our commitment to mastering vocal communication can really pay dividends.

The Power of Managing Your Vocal Power

In her groundbreaking book *Radical Candor*, my friend and colleague Kim Scott tells the story of an interaction she had with Sheryl Sandberg after one of her first pitches to Eric Schmidt. She calls it "The 'Um' Story."

Kim had recently joined Google and the division she led, AdSense, was growing at an unprecedented rate. She pitched Eric about some ideas she had for her division's continued growth.

Afterward, Sheryl gave Kim several clear and specific compliments on the presentation, then told her, "You said 'um' a lot. Were you aware of it?" Kim dismissed this feedback, and Sheryl gave it again. Again Kim dismissed it. Sheryl brought it up a third time, and a third time Kim dismissed the feedback from her new boss.

Finally Sheryl decided to get Kim's attention. She said, "I can see I am going to have to be really, really direct to get through to you. You are one of the smartest people I know, but saying 'um' so much makes you sound stupid." *That* got Kim's attention!

She listened, got coaching, and solved the issue. Kim uses this story to show the power of radical candor, and I love it because it underscores how very senior people, like Sheryl Sandberg, do indeed notice if you don't have strong vocal power.

Visual: What They See

Our discussion so far gives you a sense of the verbal and the vocal, but remember the suggestion we started with: More than half of what we communicate is non-verbal—neither in what we say or how we say it, but in what we are not saying: through our body language, our mannerisms, and the way we use the space and items around us. This includes your eye contact, your facial expressions, your gestures, the way you sit, stand, or move, or even the way you're dressed. Anything the audience sees makes up the visual component of your communication.

We want to focus on five core aspects of visual communication that all great presenters should master:

- Eye contact
- Posture
- Gestures
- Physical movement
- Speaking space

First and foremost—more important than any other element we'll discuss within visual communication—is sustained, direct eye contact with the people you are addressing. It's important that speakers arrive at a place where they can feel comfortable holding four to seven seconds of direct eye contact with the audience. To get there, I offer my students the strategy of "one person, one thought." So I'll deliver one complete thought to a person on the left side of the room, and we'll actually have a moment. Then I'll turn my body and deliver another thought to a person on the right side of the room; I'll stay there long enough to truly connect with that person. Even in a short pitch of three to five minutes, if I make sure I have focused eye contact with different members of the audience—or if it's a large room, with different sections of the audience—my audience will leave feeling connected to my message. Any time I place my eyes anywhere else than on my audience—when I look at my slides, my notes, or my watch, for example—I'm giving up a value. I'm giving up an opportunity to connect.

In addition to clear, strong eye contact, a successful speaker should also have clear, strong posture. I recommend keeping your feet shoulder width apart, maybe four to six inches from each other. If you keep your feet too close together, you'll find that you look stiff, feel less stable, and are less free to move naturally. If your feet are too wide apart, you heard it here first: you're going to look a bit awkward, like a seafaring captain trying to keep balance on a boat.

My colleagues who specialize in executive presence for women have helped me to understand the distinction between how men and women should place their feet. While men's best stance has the feet form a rectangle, women (with a different center of gravity) will often find it better to have one foot slightly in front of the other, more like a diamond on the floor. Both men and women should consider having their weight evenly distributed between both feet, so as not to lean or slouch. So let's aim for the middle ground of a nice, natural stance with your hands comfortably at your sides to allow you to gesture successfully. Chapter Six contains more information on strategies specific to women leaders when they present.

Too many speakers start their presentations with their arms tucked in closely by their waists; then, when they gesture, they sometimes end up looking like the T-Rex trying to reach for prey: A for effort, but not much range. If you're able to keep your arms down by your sides, you'll find that when you do gesture, you'll naturally bring your gestures upward, offering you a bolder and more interesting range of gestures.

Depending on the environment in which you're delivering your pitch or talk, you may have the ability to incorporate physical movement into your presence, perhaps moving from one place on the stage to another. Physical movement is not only an excellent way to be more interesting to your audience, but also a useful channel for offloading some of that nervous energy you may be feeling as you present. As you start to use the space, it's important to remember to move on transitions. Offer one complete thought from one place on the stage before transitioning, walking to another place in the room, and offering your next complete thought. Not only does movement keep your audience engaged, but it can sometimes allow you to support the content you're sharing by physically demonstrating transition and breaks in material.

As you move, be aware of your speaking space: the distance between you and your audience. While different cultures have varying norms for what's appropriate, certainly a good rule of thumb is to keep at least 18 inches between yourself and the closest person in your audience. Likewise, though, you don't want to be too far from your audience, as this can make them feel disconnected from you. On the same theme, remove anything that might lie between you and your audience, since this can interfere with your connection. If there's a lectern, consider presenting from in front of it or beside it rather than behind it. Remember that your guiding principle should be connection with your audience: placing nothing between you, how can you use the space between you and your stakeholders to maximize connection?

The Most Watched Student Talk from My Teaching

As I noted in the introduction of this book, most of the work I ask students to do is individual, since that's where leaders can see the most improvement and remain the most engaged. But I do ask students to complete a final team presentation on a communication topic of their choice. I invite the teams who produce the best of these talks to let me add them to the Stanford YouTube channel.

(Continued)

Currently our Communication Lessons Playlist has about 40 titles on a range of topics. As of August 2019 the entire library had millions of views, but one title alone accounts for over 3.8 million of that number. It's entitled "Make Body Language Your Superpower." The four students who created it, Matt Levy, Collin Bailie, Jeong Joon Ha, and Jennifer Rosenfeld, love that their number of views has surpassed Oprah's talk at the GSB and continues to rise. It reinforces the thirst so many leaders have to better understand, and channel, the power of non-verbal communication.

Once you've focused attention on the verbal, the vocal, and the visual, you'll be well positioned to speak about your ideas or deliver your pitch. Later on, we'll dive in to some special topics that may supplement your tool kit: considerations around setting, context, or special types of communication. But everyone who has invested in optimizing their verbal offerings, their vocal delivery, and their visual presentation is ready to speak successfully.

A Few Words on Derailers

In her book *The Credibility Code*, Cara Hale Alter identifies four "derailers" that often detract from the effectiveness of our presentations or interactions. Three of them inform how we speak our messages aloud. In the early weeks of our Strategic Communication course at the GSB, students review Alter's

(Continued)

derailers in detail. We're including these here so you can consider them in your plan for upholding credibility and letting
your audience focus on your message.

Filler Words

While it isn't, um, so much that filler words are negative in
and of themselves, too many filler words can, um, distract
the audience from your, uh, message, and make it hard for
them to retain information. (You see where we're going with
this.) We often think of filler words as "um," "uh," or "like,"
but in fact filler words are any words that don't add meaning to the sentence you're speaking. We use them when
we're searching for the next word, when we're nervous, or
when we're unsure. So it's no wonder that when the audience hears these words, they begin to think of us as timid
or unsure.

Eliminating filler words need not be a perfect system. Certainly, when we're talking with friends, chatting on the phone
with family, or ordering our morning coffee, there's no need to
panic when an errant "um" sneaks in. But having the ability to
eliminate or at least minimize filler words in high-stakes situations is a skill worth cultivating.

Alter recommends starting by cultivating your awareness
around filler words; most of us aren't aware that we use them,
or of how often we do so. As we will describe in more detail
later, the best way to gain some perspective on your patterns
is to watch yourself on video. (Painful, we know—but worth
the payoff!) This could be as simple as having a friend use your
phone to record your response to simple questions about your

(Continued)

interests, passions, or projects. Try to speak for at least two minutes to get the full benefit.

You may be surprised at what you hear, or where you find yourself reaching to use a filler word instead of a content-rich one. Once you're aware of your filler word usage, you might try pausing in place of filler words. In general, slowing down your speech will make it easier to choose your words deliberately.

Uptalk

Alter also warns of "uptalk," that phenomenon where we end every statement as though it were a question. While asking a well-placed question can certainly be a show of great strength, nobody wants to be perceived as unsure when we're delivering a message that matters to us or making a definitive statement. That "question impression" happens when our tone rises at the end of a turn of speaking.

To improve your credibility, try starting from a higher tone and moving down to a lower tone. This is particularly important when you're introducing yourself or talking about your credentials. When students are preparing or revising a presentation, I recommend that they pay special attention to their downward tone when they're talking about their value proposition or experience—the places where you should exhibit the most confidence and security in who you are and what you do. Sometimes the internal mantra "end with a period, not a question mark" can further reinforce this strategy.

To become familiar with this, leaders can visualize or even demonstrate with their hands the difference between going up

(Continued)

(hand soaring up and to the right as you get higher) and going down (hand moving slowly down and to the left). Visualizing this exercise can go a long way to reducing uptalk effectively.

Self-Commenting

There's no one among us who hasn't said a word we didn't mean to say, tripped over a misplaced computer cord on the way to the stage, or searched too long for just the right phrase. But commenting unnecessarily on these slipups can undermine our credibility even further.

Rather than apologize or acknowledge our momentary errors—whether it be cracking a joke at our own expense, assuring the audience we're about to get right on track, flinching, or offering an uncomfortable facial expression, I urge students to try to simply keep going.

Experiment with what it feels like to maintain a neutral facial expression, even vocal tone, and to avoid remarking on the parts of your messaging that aren't your favorites. Chances are, if the audience notices them, they will notice these moments far less than the announcement of them a moment later.

3 Writing for Impact: Active, Brief, and Clear

When I teach business writing, I often tell students that their writing will go further in the organization than they will. The email you write will be read by the CEO before you ever meet. More people will see your slide deck than will ever sit in an audience at your presentation. Writing matters more than ever now in business, and yet it's one of the hardest things to get people to focus on. Why is that? In a world of quick communication, we often forget that one of the most powerful tools for scaling our leadership is the written word. And for many of us, the stakes feel higher when we're writing—not only because our words often enter the room before we do and stay after we've left—but because writing commits our thoughts to paper in a way that feels definite. Well, writing is high-stakes. But that doesn't mean it has to be confining, difficult, or isolating. The best writing represents you in a way that feels as authentic as a conversation and connects you to an audience beyond your immediate circle.

I like to start with the building blocks of business writing: the ABCs. All business writing should be Active, Brief, and Clear.

Active

I urge my students to adjust their writing to the active voice whenever and wherever possible. This usually requires two steps: First, we have to be able to identify the passive voice in our writing. Second, we have to replace the passive voice with something more energetic and engaging. The distinction between these two sentences easily illustrates the distinction between passive (1) and active (2) voice:

1. The ball was kicked by Tim.
2. Tim kicked the ball.

The active sentence puts the protagonist at the beginning of the sentence. It more immediately answers the question, "Who did what?" Not only is that sentence more concise and engaging, but it gives credit to Tim. Consider how easily the first sentence might be shortened to "The ball was kicked," completely eliminating Tim from the equation. (And after all the hard work he put in!) There are plenty of examples of the passive voice as weak communication through history and pop culture. Think of Reagan's notorious "Mistakes were made," or "Recommendations were offered," or "Opinions were expressed."

It's not that we should never use the passive voice, but we should limit its use to keep our writing active and engaging. In high school I had a remarkable instructor, Mr. Dave Wessling, who drilled into us the ironic phrase, "The passive voice is that which is to be avoided." When we write using the passive voice, we can come across as pompous, arrogant, or at the very least, out of touch with the situation we're trying to describe. We downgrade the human element of our communication—and it's the human element to which our audiences most strongly connect.

Committing to the active voice enables us to be distinct from other writers in the organization and is the first step toward stronger business writing.

The closest my classes ever come to resembling high-school grammar classes is when I teach the concept of eliminating concealed verbs. Here, I illustrate the process by which we take a lovely active verb and tack on an ending like -ion or -tion to turn it into a noun. "We decided" becomes "We made a decision." "We informed the stakeholders" becomes "We gave the stakeholders some information." When we can eliminate these camouflaged verbs and use the verbs themselves, our writing becomes more active and more interesting—not to mention that we naturally position ourselves to be more concise.

Another way to amplify your active writing is to avoid the faulty subject structures "it is" and "there are." When we see those phrases, we don't know what "it" or "there" refers to. As I was creating my own doctorate dissertation at Penn, my advisor went through one entire chapter, circling each time I used one of these constructions. At times the subject was clear, but most of the time the subject was not identifiable. (I was so focused on my research that my active writing voice slipped into unconscious incompetence mode!) These constructions are so easy to identify in a draft. If you are able to transform even half of them into more active, clear, and interesting sentences, you will improve your document immensely.

Brief

The attention spans of our readers are likely not what we would hope them to be. At best, they are unpredictable. Again I rely on Mr. Wessling, who famously told our class, "Make your answers long enough to finish." As a leader, each of us wants to be known as someone whose message is clear, concise, and unambiguous, and it takes time to write that way. But if we invest the time, our readers won't have to. And it's far more likely that they will make it through our document, grasp our message, and remember it.

Try eliminating weak verbs like *is, was, were, has, have,* and *had.* Using a more powerful verb (see our list in Appendix A) creates a more engaging sentence that requires fewer words. You might also try reducing a phrase to a single word. "Made a decision" could become "decided." "Came into the room" could be "arrived."

And in the interest of our own brevity . . . we'll leave it at that.

Clear

If you've succeeded in writing actively and briefly, your writing should now be clear. To make sure, think back to the AIM framework. Ask yourself: After reading this document, will the audience take the action I want them to take? Is it clear what I'm asking them to do? Is there any thought, phrase, or sentence that will cause the reader to stumble? If there's a point in an email where a reader has to re-read a paragraph for clarity, it's not the reader's failing—it's the writer's.

At the end of this section, we'll offer you some ways to edit others' writing as well as your own. There you'll find a number of other strategies to determine whether your writing is active, brief, and clear enough to make the impact you want.

Synthesis > Summary

When I teach writing, I begin by adapting a technique I first learned in Chip and Dan Heath's *Made to Stick.* They relate a story from the legendary screenwriter Nora Ephron (famous for the films *Silkwood, When Harry Met Sally,* and *Julie & Julia,* to name just a few). When Ephron was a student in high school, her journalism instructor gave the class the facts below and asked them to write the headline:

> Kenneth L. Peters, the principal of Beverly Hills High School, announced today that the entire high school faculty will travel to Sacramento next Thursday for a colloquium in new teaching methods.

Among the speakers will be anthropologist Margaret Mead, college president Dr. Robert Maynard Hutchins, and California governor Edmond 'Pat' Brown.

(Made to Stick, p. 75)

I put that same task in front of my MBA students, asking them to come up with a headline for a high school newspaper based on these facts. Much like Ephron's peers decades ago, my students end up summarizing the facts, without much style. In fact, many times their headline is simply a repetition of the facts I gave them.

The job of a headline writer is not to summarize, but rather to synthesize: capture the essence of the information for the audience at hand. In this case, as Ephron's wise journalism instructor told them, the headline should be "No School Next Thursday." That's the core message for the audience reading the paper.

Any manager can summarize, but it's the task of a leader to synthesize. That's why I tell them the one (and only) formula they will ever need to know is Syn>Sum. Synthesis is greater than summary. It's a crucial skill to learn.

Our colleague Matt Abrahams gets at the same point with this structural tip: When you're delivering a message, think, "What, so what, now what." Share the information (what), tell us why it's relevant (so what), and articulate what action is needed (now what). It's another pithy way to emphasize that leadership communication delivers information that allows the audience to quickly grasp the action that's required. Synthesis is a crucial, and often ignored, leadership skill. Any manager can synthesize (what), but it's the task of a leader to synthesize (so what, now what).

Another way we get to the difference between synthesis and summary is this technique we use in the LOWKeynotes program, where GSB students deliver a "half TED talk" of nine minutes to a large audience. During the iteration period for these talks, students deliver rehearsals to a small group of peers, guest coaches, and faculty like myself. As the students deliver their talks, I type furiously on my iPad. I write down every thought I have: what's working, what isn't, questions that could be answered, visuals that could be included. But to bombard the speaker with this summary of every thought I have would be overwhelming . . . and difficult to prioritize. So rather than offering a summary—a comprehensive brain dump of every suggestion—I distill my summary down to a synthesis. I offer the top points for the speaker to take away: a few things that worked, and a few places to focus for the next iteration. Think of your summary as the full overview and your synthesis as the highlights—and aim to offer the latter.

The Yin and Yang of Writing: Style and Content

Whenever I teach business writing, I show students a picture of a yin-and-yang symbol. I encourage them to think of the yin as the style and format, and the yang as the substance and content. Each is of equal weight. If your report is informative and substantive, but written in an unengaging style, no one will read it and it won't have impact. If your email is beautifully formatted and styled but lacks substance, it won't persuade your reader. To be a successful writer, you can't have one without the other. There has to be a *there* there.

When your writing is active, brief, and clear and you're offering syntheses rather than summaries, you're well on your way to persuasive, meaningful substance and content. Turning your attention to style and format requires you to focus on making your document user-friendly. The easier it is for your readers to navigate and digest your words, the more they'll appreciate your message. In the words of the SEC's *Plain English Handbook*, "A plain English document is easy to read and looks like it's meant to be read" (5).

A good place to start is at the very beginning of your document. From the title of your report or the subject line of your email, your reader should already know your main point, ask, or argument. Consider your title as a TL;DR. How many of us have skipped over an email with the uninformative subject line, "Checking in," "Following up," or, even less informative, "No subject"? Your readers are more likely to read on (or open the attachment) if they know why they are doing it. Some better versions of the subject lines above might be "Rescheduling August 22 meeting" or "Follow-up chat about design on Friday 11 a.m.?" These subject lines cut right to the chase. They're descriptive, precise, and they let the reader know why you've composed the document.

Once you've opened with an informative title, continue the theme by using actionable headings. Each section of your document should begin with a bold, specific, and actionable heading with your key takeaway. If busy readers were to skip all of the body paragraphs of your document and read only title and headings, they should be able to understand your main arguments and asks. To decide on your heading, identify the main thing a reader should know about that section of your email or report. Then format it as a bolded phrase at the top of that section.

Now you might think about how your document looks. Is it a sea of words without much white space? How often are you giving your reader the respite of a paragraph break? Adding ample white space to your document allows your reader a rest to digest your message. It can make your document feel more approachable. Try looking at your document as though it were a piece of art. What's the ratio of white space to words? See whether you can increase that ratio to improve the readability of your document.

One way to improve that ratio is by using bullet points. Bullet points increase your use of white space, highlight important terms, and can clearly visualize lists. We urge our students to look for lists or itemized points in their documents, and where appropriate, experiment with using bullet points to express those lists. The easier it is to scan your email or report, the better.

A Brief Note on Slidedocs

In the years since I first began teaching business writing we've seen an astounding evolution in the way slides are used. For many years, the major consulting firms produced large decks of information for their clients, using PowerPoint as more of word-processing tool than a presentation tool. For a while I fought this trend, criticizing the management consultants in my classes for cluttering slides with too many words. However, I came to realize that the walking deck—slides as deliverables—was not only a trend I could not buck, but a valuable opportunity for teaching good writing and visual display of information.

My realization was reinforced in 2016 when my presentation hero, Nancy Duarte, and her team registered "slidedoc" with a trademark and provided a remarkable free resource on their website at http://www.duarte.com/slidedocs/. This 165-slide PDF file is truly meta: a slidedoc on how to create slidedocs. Here Duarte defines a slidedoc as "a document created using presentation software, where visuals and words unite to illustrate one clear point per page. The result is a medium that can be read and digested more quickly than either a document or a presentation. Slidedocs are meant to be printed and distributed or read on screen without the accompaniment of a presenter."

I cannot recommend this item highly enough. Quite simply: it rocks. The Duarte team has provided clear direction and easy-to-follow templates on their website.

The Power of Editing (Others' Work and Your Own)

This section of our book isn't about the rules of grammar. It's about leadership writing, which focuses on results and intent. And the best chance you can give yourself to write for impact (in a way that's active, brief, and clear!) is to invest in your skills as an editor. Taking a second or third look not only at your own work, but at the work of others, can improve your ability to spot opportunities for concision and clarity. With enough practice, good editors will be able to spot the patterns of bad habits in their own work, and over time, they'll be able to eliminate more of these habits on the first pass.

But as you start writing, our hope is that you'll relieve yourself of the burden of editing. Per Anne Lamott in *Bird by Bird*, we hope that your first attempt at writing your email, report, or presentation will truly be a "shitty first draft." Think of your drafting period as a time to get out all your thoughts with your audience, intent, and message in mind. Most of us are much more effective editors with the benefit of distance from the document. When you're finished writing your shitty first draft, get up, stretch your legs, have some coffee. You've earned it. Then, in an hour—or even better, in a day—return to your document with fresh eyes, armed with the following set of recommendations for evaluating your work.

Through her extensive experience as a coach at the GSB and beyond, my coauthor Kara Levy has developed a specific approach to coaching editing that I want to share here for you. Kara says:

> First, I urge my students to read their work back to themselves aloud. The ear will often catch errors or habits that the eye can't. While reading, our eyes do us the magical service of filling in blanks where words are missing, interpreting awkward constructions for us, and traversing long blocks of text that could (and should!) be much shorter. But our ears are not so talented. When we read our work aloud, we find out

how long it takes us to read a lengthy sentence or how many times we've repeated a word. So find a place where you won't disturb your neighbors or garner odd looks from your colleagues, and start by reading your work aloud.

For your own work and for others' work, pay close attention to where you want to know more. When questions come up, mark them. What kind of information would satisfy your curiosity? Would a reason make the point stronger? Would an example illustrate the reason more fully?

Where do you get confused, bored, or otherwise thrown off track? Likewise, it can be helpful to mark where you find the prose especially energetic, the points well made, or the conversation interesting. Reinforcing what's working is a useful way to create habits around writing tendencies that contribute to our success.

Return to the suggestions we've made about being active, brief, and clear; and about considering structure. Have you done so effectively?

Next, you may want to listen—remember, we're still reading aloud here—for a few specific opportunities to tighten and strengthen your prose. Here are some places to begin:

- **Avoid conditionals.** Where you hear "I would suggest," change the phrase to "I suggest."

- Remember the active part of "active, brief, and clear." **Where you hear the passive voice, convert it to active voice.**

- **Where you see a long phrase communicating an action, reduce it to a single verb**. For example, "makes you feel motivated to" could simply be "inspires."

- **Remove information that the audience already knows.** This could be something as factual as data with which the audience is already familiar, or as sneaky as the phrase "I think." (Your readers already assume that you hold these opinions, since you are their author!)

- **Break a long sentence into two or more.** You'll know if the sentence is long if you had to take a big breath in the middle, if it took effort to parse, or if you got confused midway.

- **Remember the power of informative titles and headings.** Try the scan test: If you read only the title and your headings of your document and skipped the body paragraphs, would you understand the general message, ask, or argument? If not, it might be a good time to add some specific and informative language to your title and headings.

Trading work with a colleague or friend can help you to familiarize yourself with applying these tools to others' writing styles as well as your own. And those extra minutes you spend ensuring that your writing is as active, brief, and clear as it needs to be can improve your impact and increase your credibility in ways that may make the difference between a convincing document and a forgettable one. Think of editing as a gift you give yourself twice: the freedom to write a first draft unburdened by correctness, and the opportunity to use perspective to craft your best work.

Glenn Kramon's Winning Writing

I was originally hired at Stanford to create a writing program to accompany the CAT (Critical Analytical Thinking) course, launched in the fall of 2007. I worked with a team of talented writing coaches for eight years. Each fall we reviewed between 2,000 and 4,000 papers and provided detailed feedback and individual coaching opportunities. But in all those years, with all those hours, and with a remarkable group of talented coaches, we never achieved the impact and appetite for writing that just one man did.

In the fall of 2014 Glenn Kramon joined the GSB faculty as a lecturer in marketing and created an elective called Winning Writing. In just a few quarters, the demand for his class was so

(Continued)

high that he had to add more sections. In a few years, he was moved to a full-time role. Currently he teaches nearly 40 percent of the GSB student body each year (and a few PhDs and grad students from other schools). The hallmark of his classes is his unique blend of wry wit and rich personalized feedback.

At the end of each term he provides a synthesis of all the lessons he has imparted, complete with before/after examples from student work submitted that term. Like many of my colleagues at the GSB, he's generously allowed me to provide a few of his lessons below for my readers.

"You can demonstrate that you're an inspiring and constructive leader by how you write, not just by how you speak. So, no matter what you're writing—an email, feedback, a performance review—remember to praise, and talk constructively.

"Say what you like, and what you *would* like. Not what you don't like. Otherwise, no one will listen. As my colleague Tom Friedman wrote in his October 2, 2002, *New York Times* column:

> There are two kinds of critics in life, those who criticize you because they want you to fail, and those who criticize you because they want you to succeed. And people can smell the difference a mile away. If you convey to people that you really want them to succeed, they will take any criticism you dish out. If you convey that you really hold them in contempt, you can tell them that the sun is shining and they won't listen to you.

"Avoid destructive words like 'this is boring' or 'this is irrational.' Instead, say how to make it better. That's the most important lesson from 'Winning Writing.'"

In Appendix C, you can find even more from Glenn. His entire course summary is posted on my website at http://www.jdschramm.com/mastery.

Part 2 Tailoring Your Communication to Goal, Setting, or Identity

4 Tailoring Your Communication to Your Goal

Though you should always consider your intent when you're crafting a communication, sometimes you can build on that exercise by using specific media, formatting, language, or information ordering to meet specific goals. The more measurable and specific your goal, the better you'll be able to customize your communication to meet the needs of your audience. Here are some of the most frequent use cases we encounter at Stanford and beyond.

Pitching

Any time we try to gain buy-in for an idea, even one as simple as where to meet a friend for lunch, we're pitching: proposing the merit of an idea for others' support and collaboration. But in this chapter, we're going to focus on the type of pitching that challenges entrepreneurs every day: pitching your business venture or collaboration. From the thousands of pitches we have seen at the GSB and beyond, we've gathered our best tips for creating meaningful, memorable content and for tightening your message to engage your audience. We'll lead you through identifying the problem your idea is solving, the solution you're offering, the market you're targeting, and the business you're planning. Then I'll give you a step-by-step look at a pitching exercise I offer my students to refine their message for presentation.

Creating Your Pitch Content: Problem, Solution, Market, and Business

For as long as I've been teaching presentation skills—and I confess it's been quite a long time—I've encouraged entrepreneurs to start with content when creating an engaging, memorable pitch. I think one of the finest resources out there right now about creating pitch content is Chris Lipp's *The Startup Pitch*. Chris has taken a survey of the thousands of pitches he's seen here in Silicon Valley and beyond to analyze what exactly entrepreneurs include to ensure an effective pitch. From that analysis, he's devised a very simple four-part structure to an effective pitch (Figure 4.1).

First, we must convince the audience of the problem. Then, we have to present our solution—and its direct connection to the details of the problem we've just outlined. Next, we must demonstrate that there's a market for solving this problem. It's not simply that *we* have a problem parking in downtown San Francisco, for example, but that *many* people share this San Francisco parking problem . . . and that many cities share this issue and would benefit from the solution we're offering. (And not only would they benefit, but they'd pay for that solution!) Finally, we need to demonstrate that we have a viable business model: that by solving this problem for this market,

Figure 4.1 Chris Lipp's pitch formula
Source: From *Startup Pitch* by Chris Lipp. SpeakValue 2014.

your investors stand to receive revenue. Whether that model is an ad model, a subscription model, direct sales, or B2B sales, we need to demonstrate that we have a clear plan to extract value.

Let's look individually at each of these four areas.

Problem   As you begin by describing the problem, it's important to describe it clearly, making sure that your audience understands the pain of the problem. Why is this such an issue? What are the repercussions of this problem and why do they matter? If the problem is familiar and widespread, it may not take you long to establish the stakes. But if the problem is lesser known or more nuanced, you may need to share video, graphs, or testimonies about why it needs to be solved. Raise the stakes by noting any trends you see for this problem. Is it getting worse as the population ages? Do environmental, economic, or time-based factors increase its impact over time? If that's true, then you can make the point that the need for your solution will only increase over time. Be sure that your audience understands the immediacy of the problem before you move on to phase two: your solution.

Solution   Chris Lipp opens his conversation of solution by addressing the importance of your USP, or unique selling proposition. Why are you able to solve this issue in a way that others haven't been able to yet? What's going to set your startup apart from anyone else who's trying to work in that space? In other words: why you, why this, why now?

If you have the opportunity to lead us through a demo of your solution, or to take us to your app or your site, the benefits of that hands-on experience with your offering can only serve your pitch.

Finally, be sure that you talk about the benefits of your solution to your stakeholders. Make sure we understand why your solution to this problem will be of use *to us*, your audience. Too often people are tempted to speak only about the features of their product, but they're leaving out an important pitching factor when they do so. Think of Steve Jobs introducing the iPod Nano: He didn't tell us it had 16GB of memory or that it was two inches wide by three inches deep. Instead, he said, "Imagine a thousand songs in your pocket." He described the features of the iPod Nano by talking about the benefit to the user. Outlining the benefits of your solution is absolutely crucial to gaining investment in your product.

Market   As you move your focus to market concerns, you'll want to talk about the initial target market you've identified as well as any expansions you anticipate beyond that initial market. Share an estimate of the market size. Here's where you demonstrate to us that you've done your research—not only about what the market is, but what potential it holds. As you discuss the market, you'll want to effectively capture the advantages of serving this market of consumers that you're targeting. Perhaps this is a group of high-net-worth individuals to whom other products could be introduced. Perhaps this is an underserved market for whom your offering could be a gateway to other products and services. Be certain that you establish not only that you know your market well, but that serving the market you have in mind offers explicit benefits.

Business   Last, you'll want to cover the details of the business itself. What is your go-to-market strategy? Specifically, you'll want to share when and how you're planning to bring this product or service to the market. It's important to share your model for earning revenue and to offer some clarity around when you think that revenue model will begin to be profitable for you. Familiarize your investors with some milestones at which they could expect to see some return on their investment.

■■■

As I look at this model—Problem, Solution, Market, Business—I often think of it as a baseball diamond. First, I have to get to first base, where I explain the problem and convince investors that the problem needs to be solved. Second base is where I reveal my solution to this problem: my unique selling proposition. Third base: There is a market for this solution, an opportunity that needs to be captured. But the home run, where we score an investor, is demonstrating that I have a business model that will capture revenue to serve this market, offering a solution to this problem.

How much time you spend on each of these components depends on the familiarity and intricacy of the problem you're solving and the solution you're offering, and the context that your investors already possess. You'll customize the proportion of time you spend on each element, depending on the concerns of your business and the level of knowledge that your audience has. But I urge you not to skip any of these important steps. They work together to offer your audience a clear picture of why they should help you to bring your idea to life.

Building the Bridge: An Exercise to Tighten Your Pitch

Much of the pitch work I've done at Stanford has been with teams of entrepreneurs preparing to deliver a pitch together. Most of this has been through Stanford's highly successful Ignite Program, started by Garth Saloner and now led by Yossi Feinberg. This certificate program is offered on campus in the summer as a full-time four-week session and in the winter as a part-time three-month experience. Each summer, we also invite a group of military veterans to campus for a tailored version of Ignite, addressing their distinct needs as they transition from the military to civilian life as entrepreneurs.

In these team settings, one participant acts as the "idea generator"—the person who proposes the product or innovation for the entire team's work, from the creation of the business plan to the pitch.

I visit the participants early in the course to provide the basics of effective pitching; then, about a week before their final pitches to an invited group of VCs, I return to provide coaching for the teams.

These coaching sessions serve as a gating function for the teams. Almost always, it's clear that few groups have actually rehearsed as a team before meeting me. They often present five or six "individual presentations" on the same topic. There may be a clear delegation of duties, but not a sense of cohesion. They've worked in silos to prepare the material. Some teams even show "frankendecks"—a slide deck stitched together with inconsistent formatting, colors, and fonts, giving a sense that the presentation is not a single entity, but rather a collection of mismatched parts. While the pitches are rocky in this state, they're certainly not without potential. Walking through my bridge exercise often helps create the alignment needed (Figure 4.2).

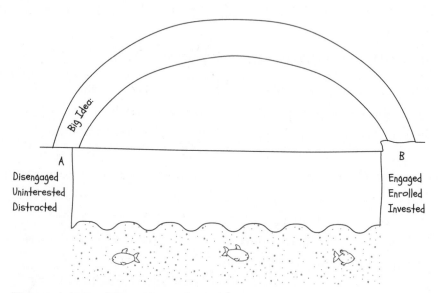

Figure 4.2 Building the bridge, no pillars

To begin, I approach a full whiteboard in the classroom. On the left side, I draw one bank of a river and on the right, the opposite bank. I start on the left side, explaining, "This is Point A, where your investors begin: disengaged, uninformed, potentially even resistant."

Then I move to the far right side: "And here is Point B, where you want them to arrive: engaged, enrolled, committed, maybe even 'invested' in the idea so much that they open their address books or checkbooks to help you succeed. To get from Point A to Point B, you need to construct a bridge through your team presentation to get them across the river."

Next I draw the arch supports stretching from Point A to Point B. The arch represents the "big idea" for the innovation. I ask the students, "If you had to synthesize the pitch into seven to eleven words, few enough to fit on a billboard, what would you say?" We wordsmith for a while on this and ultimately settle on a working theme for the pitch that encompasses problem, solution, and opportunity. That idea becomes the bridge connecting Point A to Point B (Figure 4.3).

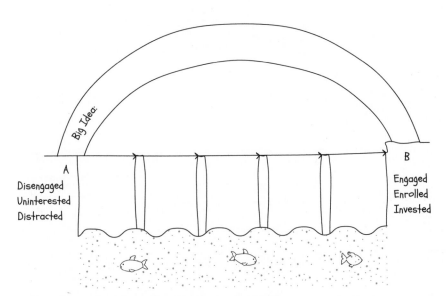

Figure 4.3 Building the bridge, with pillars

Still, even with a bridge scaffold from A to B, we need a platform on which to walk from one side to the other. Each speaker provides a "little idea," which edges us from the first words of the pitch (capturing attention) to the final words of the pitch (inviting participation). In this portion of the activity, students begin to see how their pieces connect to the others. Team members will begin to trade content elements with one another. This more holistic view of the presentation starts to take on value.

Figure 4.4 shows one example of a bridge completed by 2019 Veterans Ignite Program team. They generously allowed me to use this to illustrate the concept. A team of six came together around one member's startup idea, Amissa, an innovative wearable device to help track Alzheimer patients who've wandered away. Jon Corkey, a 25-year Navy veteran, founded the firm based in Charlotte, North Carolina. After beginning the startup process on his own, he

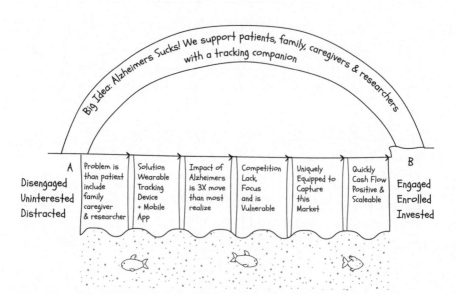

Figure 4.4 Building the bridge, totally filled out but no CTA

came to Stanford to flesh it out more fully and build his skills as an entrepreneur. Once I had sketched out the bridge exercise on the whiteboard, Jon's team struggled to define the big idea or overarching theme for the presentation. Usually, I try to encourage a team to capture the essence of this theme in seven to eleven words (like a billboard or bumper sticker). We settled on "Alzheimer's sucks! We support patients, families, caregivers, and researchers with a tracking companion."

Next I went to each member of the team and asked them to similarly articulate the "little idea" that they were contributing to the larger presentation. Each little idea would fit into the big idea with the same constraints (Figure 4.4).

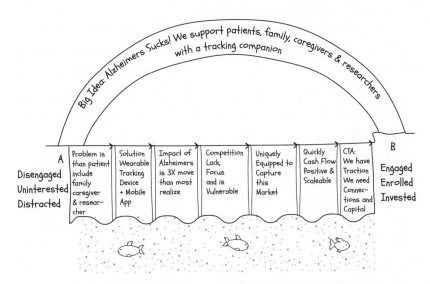

Figure 4.5 Building the bridge, totally filled out with CTA

But the real magic came when Jon synthesized his closing call to action, which connects the bridge back to the other shore (Figure 4.5): "We have traction. We need contacts and capital to succeed."

A few days after our work together, the Amissa team delivered their final pitch to a group of VCs who found the team's work and Jon's innovation impressive. The team shared with me that the bridge helped them to be more compelling and more cohesive. Jon's now back in North Carolina pursuing the venture even further. You can follow his progress at Amissa.com.

Pitching on CUE: Curiosity, Understanding, and Evangelism

Before we end this section on pitching, there's one final framework you may find helpful. Our colleague Burt Alper, who teaches pitching in several settings, reminds his entrepreneurs to remember the acronym CUE. He suggests that all pitches have three primary segments: curiosity, understanding, and evangelism.

During the curiosity phase, an entrepreneur should capture the audience's attention. Make the potential investors or partners curious, ideally dying to know more. You can achieve this curiosity by presenting compelling research, asking insightful questions, or sharing vivid stories. However you decide to do so, draw your audience in and inspire them to want to know more.

The next stage, Burt explains, is where you must create understanding. You might create understanding by providing technical details, sharing sketches, or conducting a demo of your product. Standing on the platform you've built in the first phase, you must explain the innovation in a clear and simple fashion so that your audience truly understands it.

But creating curiosity and providing understanding is not enough. The third phase is to inspire the audience to become evangelists. He advises entrepreneurs to talk about future potential, massive scale, or significant value the product or service will provide. You want to create a reaction like "I can't wait to tell my partners about this" in the minds of those you pitch. As we have shared elsewhere in this book, you'll be most effective if you can "sell" in a way that feels authentic to you, yet still effective for the situation. Don't hesitate to "ask for the order." Invite the listeners to take an action that moves them closer to being engaged and enrolled.

If you have made your audience curious, allowed them to understand your proposition, and evangelized through a clear ask, you will have met the main criteria of a successful pitch. If this pared-down model appeals, consider the CUE model another tool in your pitching toolbox.

Storytelling

At bedtime, I tell my children Roma and Joshua stories. No matter how many stories I tell them, they always ask for "just one more." Even from a young age, it seems we're hard-wired to enjoy a well-told story—and for good reason. As adults, we know that stories can do the work that other types of language can't. Sometimes stories are the best way to persuade, to activate emotions, or to illustrate an important point. And they're also a way to connect with audiences through the personal, the visual, the surprising, and the memorable details we share.

Whether you're telling a story in a presentation, a business meeting, or at a networking event, the principles of good storytelling remain the same. Over our years teaching future leaders how to connect through story, we've identified some best practices that will help you make sure that your story moves people, holds their interest, and makes your message stick.

Crafting Your Story

Remember that every good story charts a change—even a subtle one—in the conditions, attitude, actions, or feelings of the characters. What is the change your story charts? "We changed our environmental practices" is not yet a story, because it doesn't reveal any change.

But "We were using three hundred plastic straws a day. One day, we saw a presentation on the effect of our waste. Then we changed our practice and eliminated plastic straws completely" is indeed a story (if a bare-bones one!). It shows a change over time. Once you're clear on the change your story reveals, experiment with how the techniques below can bring your story to life.

Parachute in   The best storytellers drop us right into the action without preamble. Rather than starting with, "I'd like to tell you a story about a time when I . . . ," place us directly in the scene of action to set the tone for the story. You can include your takeaways and learned lessons later in the narrative.

Choose your first and final words carefully   Just as you'll parachute in with a hook that grabs the audience's attention, you'll want to conclude your story with an image, reflection, or call to action that leaves them thinking about your story after it's done. Be intentional when choosing your opening and your closing.

Follow the "Goldilocks Theory" of details   Not too many, not too few. If you offer us too many details, we may get lost, or worse, bored. If you don't offer enough details, we may lack the context to grasp the story fully or to see ourselves inside your tale. Here are some of the tips Kara and I often share for how to get just the right amount of detail.

To offer less detail: Look for descriptors that are doing the same work and see whether you can eliminate doubles. Is the room both "crowded" and "claustrophobic"? These words are telling you the same information about how the room feels. Doubles can describe how something looks, feels, tastes, sounds, or smells—keep an eye out for them, and limit yourself to just one of each category for every item you're describing.

To offer more detail: Use the five senses. Is there a spot in your story where you see a lack of detail? Ask yourself, "How did this look, sound, smell, taste, feel?" You can also ask yourself, "What was the main character thinking at this moment?" These questions are prompts that may help you to populate your story with details that will help your reader connect.

Know your why   A good story has a job to do: it illustrates a point, convinces someone of an idea, or reveals something true. *Why* are you telling the story you're telling? What do you hope your audience will know or feel as a result? Think of this part of your brainstorming process as the "I tell you this because . . ." section. Often, in a business context, it's valuable to articulate to the audience what you want their takeaway to be. But whether you choose to share the takeaway verbally or not, it's essential to know the takeaway yourself. If you need a place to start, you can return, as always, to the AIM framework.

Delivering Your Story

From our conversation about verbal, vocal, and visual communication, you know that crafting your story's narrative is only part of the storytelling opportunity. A great storyteller also considers how to deliver the story to best effect, capturing and holding the audience's attention throughout.

Focus your delivery on "one person with one thought"   When speaking to a group, focus on one person at a time, for four to seven seconds. As you tell your story, try to connect with each individual if possible. Don't wash your eye contact over the crowd like a lighthouse, but actually connect with individuals. Consider even "casting" a member of the audience as a character in your story as you tell it.

Consider the power of poetry   Use fewer words to carry more meaning. My high school English teacher, Mr. Wessling, used the analogy of the "magic grain truck" to educate us about poetry. He invited us to imagine: What if a magic truck allowed a farmer to haul seven times the amount of grain that a normal truck usually holds? (Can you tell I grew up in Kansas?) We developed a long list of benefits such a truck would provide: fewer trips, less fuel, more free time. Then he concluded: "Well, that's what poetry is. Using just a few carefully chosen and arranged words to carry much more meaning than their usual weight." That imagery from over three decades ago reminds me of the power of poetry.

Use silence for impact and emphasis   When a composer writes the score for a symphony, she places a rest in the music when silence is called for. That rest is as much a part of the music as the notes. Silence is a powerful and underutilized storytelling tool. Intentional silence draws emphasis to what was just said or what is about to come—and allows others to contribute their own interpretations.

The Power of Story

We've shared extensively about the LOWKeynotes library throughout this book, so I truly hope you will visit the Stanford YouTube channel to view some of the great talks that exist there. Many of them have rich examples of storytelling. At my website, jdschramm.com/mastery, I have posted several examples with the specific storytelling skills those talks exhibit.

Rachael Wallach's 2017 talk, "Disrupting Disability," is but one example. Paralyzed at 18 after an accident, she has been an active advocate for the rights of the differently abled for years now. In the middle of her talk she shares two short stories about her experience with doctors. The first is when she was eight years old and was given a wide choice of frames to consider when she was told she'd need to wear glasses. The second is ten years later when another doctor told her she'd need to be in a wheelchair for the rest of her life. This time no choices were given to her. She ends with the haunting question, "Why can't we view people who wear their wheels like people who wear glasses?" In just a few short minutes she does everything we've covered in this chapter, from parachuting in, to the appropriate level of details, to the use of analogy, and ending with a clear finish.

Rachael has gone on to found Disrupt Disability and launched her first product, Wheelwear, a modular wheelchair you can continually customize to your body, environment, and individual style. She freely shares with others that her ability to tell stories has been key to her success as an entrepreneur.

Delivering Your Story with Data

Have you ever had the experience of seeing data that you knew you'd never be able to unsee? When that story was told so well, and the data was so rich, that you knew you'd never forget what that data meant to you? For me, that moment was in August of 1999, when my best friend, Javier, twisted my arm to get me to sign up for the Alaska AIDS Vaccine Ride. For six days, 2,500 of us rode our bikes from Fairbanks to Anchorage, Alaska, raising money for the AIDS vaccine.

The morning that we set out on our first ride, the organizers gathered us all together for an event meant to inspire us—not just to keep riding, but also to keep fundraising and collecting pledges on behalf of the vaccine long after our ride was over. As we sat there in our bike gear ready to take off, the organizers brought 34 people up onto the stage, all in jerseys bearing the logo of the ride. Twenty-eight of them were wearing black jerseys, and six of them were wearing yellow jerseys. Those 34 people represented the 34 million people affected by AIDS and HIV throughout the world at that time. The people in black jerseys represented the 28 million people in that group without access to the anti-retroviral drugs that we have access to here in the west. The six people in yellow jerseys represented the six million affected people—mostly living in the developed world—who had access to the drugs. Then 12 children stepped up onto the stage, all wearing red jerseys. These kids represented the 12 million children—mostly orphans living in Sub-Saharan Africa—who had lost both mother and father to the disease.

That example of storytelling with data still chokes me up 20 years later. And I can remember the numbers because someone was thoughtful about designing that story in a way where the numbers made a difference to me. This type of visual storytelling with data may not be available for most of the communication you do day to day, but I want to offer it as an aspirational touchpoint for thinking about what data can do for your audience when you position into an effective, compelling story.

Albert Einstein famously said, "Make everything as simple as possible, but no simpler." That's precisely what we're aiming for with the following tools for crafting data into story.

Develop the story before you develop the graphics   If you've ever seen an unintelligible slide, squinted at meaningless curves across confusing axes, or tried to make sense of what a scattergraph was trying to tell you—and we are sure you have!—you've witnessed the phenomenon of graphics preceding story. Not only is this approach hard to understand, but it fails to tell a story that will drive outcome for your audience. Thus the critical importance of developing your story *before* you develop your graphics. Think of your graphics as the tip of your communication iceberg: a tip of an iceberg represents only 10 percent of the total mass; fully 90 percent lies beneath the surface. Your graphic isn't your whole story—it's a representation of a small part of it.

So rather than starting by looking at your chart to find a story, start by looking at the *data*. Do some analysis within your idea to identify the themes, takeaways, and trends that are worth highlighting. Once I'm clear on the story I want to tell, sometimes I find it's helpful to test several different charts, graphs, or ways of visualizing the story to see which one works best.

Anytime we sit down to craft a narrative, it's valuable to consider the structure of a well-told story. In her 2011 TEDx East talk, Nancy Duarte references Freytag's pyramid to illustrate a structure I find particularly useful (Figure 4.6).

This model is over 100 years old, but we still refer to it today for good reason. It contains the most important elements of a story well told. Take a look at the beginning of the story path—notice how short the section devoted to opening and exposition is. Nine out of ten times, we don't need nearly as much windup as we think we do.

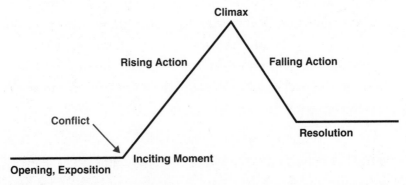

Figure 4.6 Freytag's pyramid as referenced by Nancy Duarte

Rather, we can keep the momentum of the story moving forward by moving to the central conflict as soon as possible. That conflict or inciting moment will create the action of our story, lead to its climax, and depending on what kind of story you're telling, to the falling action and the resolution.

Think of any great film you've seen in the past few decades. As a parent of a toddler, I'll admit the first movie that comes to mind is *Moana*. (Hey, it's good!) The setup of the movie is concise and the conflict arrives almost immediately: Moana's island lacks vegetation and the community doesn't have enough food. Most of the movie is devoted to the action as Moana sets out to find the all-powerful Heart of Te Fiti, finally finds it, and brings it back to her island. The quick resolution that follows shows vitality returning to the island.

This is the same kind of arc you can find in your data. What's the conflict? What's the action being taken to resolve or change the conflict? Your story may end at the climax if you're trying to get people to take action. Either way, be thoughtful about your story's arc.

Know and honor your audience   Well, here we are, back at AIM again. That's because to tell your best story, you'll need to be thoughtful about who your audience is. What's the appropriate level of data and type of illustration that will make sense to them? How sophisticated is your audience? Will they understand regression analysis? Will they be served by synthesized information, or will they appreciate having data broken down for them in a more step-by-step fashion? Think about the level of detail and sophistication you want to apply to the data you share.

Avoid the food charts (pies, donuts, and spaghetti)   The classic pie, donut, and spaghetti charts are rarely your best choice for telling a story with data, not only because, if you're like me, they're likely to make you hungry. These charts rarely format data in a way that is accessible to your audience—they make your data very difficult to interpret. Take a look at what I mean in Figures 4.7, 4.8, and 4.9.

Anyone trying to interpret the pie chart in Figure 4.7 would be hard-pressed to come up with a story. Is the bottom half of the pie chart meant to indicate some cautionary content? What should it mean? It's a lot of work to try to figure out what the presenter is telling us.

Now take the bar graph in Figure 4.8. This first bar graph shows exactly the same data, visualized differently. Can you interpret the data more easily now? You should be able to have a better sense of the takeaway your presenter has in mind when looking at the data in this different format. Especially when your data has many components or slices, you don't want to represent it in a pie, as the small visuals that result will be confusing.

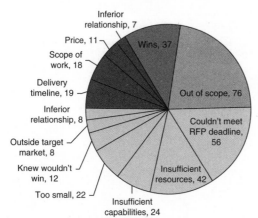

Figure 4.7 Original pie chart

Source: Storytellingwithdata.com

Timing and resource issues are top reasons we aren't submitting/winning proposals

Why we **aren't submitting** proposals

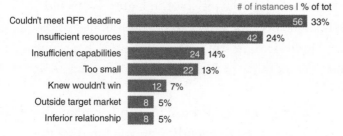

Why we **aren't winning** proposals

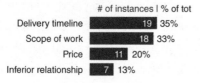

Global project summary
January–December 2015

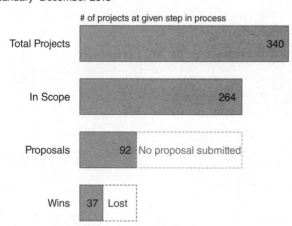

Figure 4.8 Revision showing bar chart instead
Source: Storytellingwithdata.com

Timing and Resources Prevent Proposal Success

Why we **aren't submitting** proposals

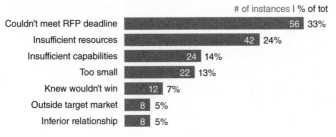

Why we **aren't winning** proposals

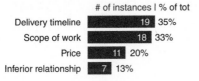

Global project summary
January–December 2015

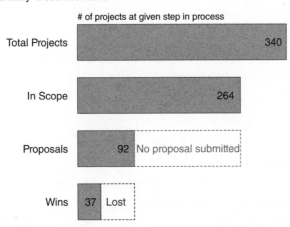

Figure 4.9 Further revision with stronger, tighter title
Source: Storytellingwithdata.com

Break a complex story into multiple slides or reveals   But you
can simplify your slides even further. That leads us to another solution to the problem of a complicated slide: consider breaking it into
multiple slides or reveals. You don't have to fit your whole story in a
single chunk. Notice how in Figure 4.8, she broke the data into three
separate pieces: "Global Project Summary," "Why we **aren't submit-
ting** proposals," and "Why we **aren't winning** proposals," making it
even easier to understand.

I've noticed that using some simple animation to dole out
information piece by piece can also make it easier for your audience to follow your story. Even if your whole team has the deck
in front of them, if you animate the slide that's up on the screen,
they'll follow the movement and be more likely to match the
pace of your story. Slowing it down can make it easier for others
to follow.

Create strong headings with power verbs   As my students well
know—and by this point in our book, you do too—I have a strong
bias against weak verbs like *is, are, was, were, has, have, had*. During
our discussion of strong writing, we covered the reasons that stronger
words can be more specific, foster concision, and inspire action. But
they're just as important when you're applying data to story, or story
to data. In Appendix A, you'll find a list of 156 power verbs that you
can use instead of these frequent offenders. Those words will inform
and compel your audience in a way that the "basic seven" can't. Most
importantly, your headings for every slide or every section of your
data should tell the story for that slide or section. Don't make your
audience do the hard work of deciphering the story from among a
cluster of unclear words—they may not be motivated or able to do so.
Be a generous presenter by offering your story in your heading using
clear language.

Simplify graphics for greater impact   When we offer the audience a complex image, we have less control over where they focus and what they take away. Keeping an image simple allows the audience to focus on the message we want them to remember. If you have backgrounds and borders, removing those is a good place to start. Eliminate legends and axis labels if possible; any time we include those, we're forcing our audience to look down or to the side, away from our central focus.

Then, go on to highlight the data point that matters. If your data story is about how bacon has the most calories of other foods in its category, consider adding a color to your bacon column, but leaving the comparison columns in gray.

Of course, the process of simplification can go too far. As we mentioned before, you do want to make things as simple as possible—but no simpler! But making a few small tweaks to the way you visually present your data can make it easier for your audience to identify the story you want it to tell.

Drill with real data   The best way for you to become proficient at storytelling with data is to practice these skills using real data. Take some data you or your company are working with right now. What stories can you uncover from the data you have? What conclusion is it leading you to draw? How could you use the techniques above to reveal those conclusions to your audience?

This is the exact assignment I offer to my students at Stanford. I break up the group into cross-functional teams and give each group an identical data set. I then provide them with an intended audience and instruct them to craft a compelling story from the data. They should illustrate that story in no more than three slides (keeping it simple!). Finally, I provide a "campfire setting" where each group shares the stories they crafted.

As with every other theme in this book, practice is what will get you closer to mastery. But practicing with real data will make your practice relevant, interesting, and unique.

Disclosing Personally

From time to time a leader may choose to share something with an audience that crosses over the line from business to personal. Steve Jobs did this when he disclosed his terminal illness. His successor, Tim Cook, did this when he chose to come out of the closet as gay. Sometimes a leader is proactive and chooses what and when to share something of a personal nature, while at other times, particularly with a scandal or misdeed, leaders don't control the narrative. There are countless examples of this in business, politics, and entertainment: Anthony Weiner, Harvey Weinstein, and Al Franken to name but a few. In fact Wikipedia has a list that runs several pages of such names.

In the LOWKeynotes program, students have chosen to share a wide range of personal facts from their own lives, ranging from struggles with depression, to sharing less visible disabilities, to being fired from their own startups, to learning of a parent's addiction to crack cocaine. I'm not sure there's a right way to do this, but I'm pretty sure many "wrong ways" exist to do this. In this section, let me provide some best practices to consider for such vulnerable self-disclosure.

No conversation about vulnerability today can begin without a reference to Brené Brown and her remarkable work on shame and vulnerability. Perhaps no individual has done more to untangle the stigma of shame from the power of vulnerability. Her initial TEDx Houston talk in 2010 has amassed over 42 million views, leading to a subsequent TED talk and a *New York Times* best-selling book, *Daring Greatly: How the Courage to Be Vulnerable Transforms the Way We Live, Love, Parent, and Lead*. If you've not read her book or seen her TED and TEDx talks, do so. They may change your life, as they have for so many others. Vulnerability is not a means to an end, but rather a choice in and of itself. If it's a choice you've made (or are weighing), consider these suggestions.

Know Your Intent and Check Your Motives

At its heart, Brown believes that vulnerability is the best treatment for shame. In *Daring Greatly* she writes: "Shame derives its power from being unspeakable." As leaders we can expand our influence if we can effectively harness the distinct power of vulnerability. Yet, proceed with caution. A leader who is trying to manipulate a team or client through "the act of vulnerability" will likely not succeed in the long run. That level of inauthenticity will, sooner or later, rise up and trip that leader. Recall the AIM model from Chapter One: "As a result of this communication what do I want the audience to think, feel, say, or do?"

If your motives for self-disclosure are self-serving, reconsider your choice to share. If, on some level, you are trying to meet a personal need by sharing, this may not be the time, place, or setting. Brown goes on to say, "I only share when I have no unmet needs I'm trying to fill. I firmly believe that being vulnerable with a larger audience is only a good idea if the healing is tied to the sharing, not to the expectations I might have for the response I get."

Share with Your Confidants First, and Take Their Counsel

It's crucial that your significant other, business partner, direct supervisor, or other key confidants know your news before you make it public. In fact, a careful conversation with such a trusted partner may be the best way to assess your intent and motivation. If people you trust and who know you well do not think it's wise to divulge the information you're considering, it may at least be worth disclosing with caution. At the extreme, you don't want these trusted people to "learn the news when everybody else finds out."

Those who've seen *Hamilton* know well the scene where Eliza learns of her husband's infidelity when he self-publishes a manuscript (the blogs of the late 1700s!) offering a political defense for the affair. While torching each love letter Hamilton ever wrote to her, Eliza sings, "In clearing your name you've ruined our lives." While dramatized for the stage, the point is well made: First, tell those you care for most. Then decide (if you have a choice), in concert with them, whether it still makes sense to share the information more widely.

Consider the Setting and the Medium

Just as you want to try to control the narrative, you likewise want to consider where and how to disclose this information. While it can be very powerful to deliver personal news in person, that may be more challenging for you and your recipients. It can be harder to process news while facing the person who is delivering it. Consider all the avenues at your disposal: handwritten note, typed email, phone call, individual meeting over a meal, small group meeting, large audience—yes, even the TED stage. If you are clear in your intent and clean with your motives, the choice of setting and medium may be fairly straightforward.

At Stanford I teach a case (written by Reynoldo Roche while an MBA student at UVA) profiling Mark Stumpp, a chief investment officer for QMA, a division of Prudential. Mark chose to undergo surgery to transition from male to female, becoming Maggie Stumpp. In 2002, when this took place, there was very little guidance for firms on how to communicate news of this kind, but Prudential did a remarkably solid job. When it was time for Maggie to return to work, her supervisor first called colleagues with close proximity to tell them the news. The supervisor called them on their home phones over the weekend before Maggie returned. Then, for other employees in the firm, a memo was sent.

Plan in Advance How to Field Questions

If you opt to deliver your information orally, you should also choose whether you will take questions about this announcement or not. If you choose to merely share in one direction, without taking questions, you should provide a resource or avenue people can use to find out more.

I vividly recall when, in January 2009, the GSB was forced to lay off over 60 people in one day due to the financial crisis. Dean Bob Joss and Senior Associate Dean Dan Rudolph were clear on this point. All of the laid-off employees were notified on a Tuesday morning before noon. At 2:00 p.m. that day, Joss and Rudolph held a town hall to share the news with everybody at the school. They provided the evidence of the loss of endowment revenue, the rationale for the cuts they made, and the process moving forward without these staff members. Yet, knowing how emotional this might be for many people, they chose to not take any questions at this time. Rather, smaller team and department meetings were set up in the coming weeks to field questions. The clarity of this choice struck me as clear and completely appropriate. You must have some way for people to pursue answers if they have questions following your disclosure.

Prepare for the Consequences

It's best to have a "best/average/worst case" plan in place before the disclosure. It's entirely possible the news may have little to no impact; it may be more valuable for you to share than for the audience to hear. Yet, it's equally possible that it will have a greater impact than you would ever have imagined. The news could go viral (literally or figuratively) and you may have many more eyes and ears in the conversation than you ever dreamed. Quite often I find that having "planned for the worst," the worst doesn't come to pass, but your confidence is heightened just knowing you have a plan.

Here, again, rely on the counsel of others. Find somebody you trust who has made a similar disclosure and see whether they can help you map out the potential ramifications. I don't know Chip Conley very well, but he took time to counsel me over the phone as I was considering doing my TED talk. He had similarly shared some of his own struggles in a TED talk and was generous, and candid, with his advice to me.

A Personal Story: My Own Journey of Self-Disclosure with My 2011 TED Talk

Many of you may have seen my TED talk, "Break the Silence for Suicide Attempt Survivors." If not, please take four minutes now and watch the talk before you read the back story of this pivotal moment in my life. While the talk went live in 2011, a few months after I delivered it, the story begins at TED 2010. There, I heard a short three-minute talk by fellow participant Glenna Fraumeni that changed my life. She shared her struggles with a malignant brain tumor and her determination to persevere despite the diagnosis. She began the talk by saying the doctors had only given her three years to live; she ended by saying, "By Christmas 2011, I will probably be gone. Where will you be?"

Her probing question haunted me. I wrote in my journal, "When will I tell my story? Maybe next year?" When it came time to register for TED 2011, I saw a separate registration for TEDYou, where leaders get a chance to deliver a talk on stage. I discussed the idea with my husband, Ken, and a trusted advisor, Roger, and decided to register to speak. As a survivor of a fairly dramatic suicide attempt in 2003 (and several smaller attempts going back as far as the seventh grade), I believed strongly that we need to be more supportive of those who've survived such an attempt on their own lives.

I worked on my talk for several weeks and, again relying on trusted advisers, hit upon the structure of telling my own story in the third person. I spoke about myself as though I were someone else, a man named John. I did not know whether I would want to reveal who John truly was. So I composed a paragraph about two and a half minutes into the four-minute talk that began, "I know John's story well because I'm John." I crafted this piece of the talk in such a way that if I chose not to, I could decide not to deliver that paragraph and the talk would still make sense. The impact would be less, but the paragraph was not necessary structurally. I had designed an "exit ramp" that I could choose to take or not take in the moment.

I prayed before walking out on stage, and knew that I would know whether to disclose when I got to that point in the talk. Today, I'm so glad that I did disclose, because I know the talk has made a much larger impact on the world with my own vulnerability visible and shame diminished. The reaction from the audience in Palm Springs was encouraging. I received a standing ovation and throughout the week people kept grabbing me for a coffee or a meal or just a hug. I was glad I disclosed.

But then TED wanted to put the talk up online. I was not sure I was ready for that much exposure. I was up for faculty reappointment at Stanford, and I didn't know how my tenured peers would feel about me admitting my struggles with depression and suicide. More urgently, I was not sure how I could face my class if the talk was seen and shared among the student body. I asked for time to decide. Even Chris Anderson himself reached out to me by email. He thoughtfully emphasized the choice was mine, saying:

> In my opinion this talk would have a big impact if we release it on ted .com. With your permission, we'd very much like to. I think you will connect with a large number of people feeling the way you once did. And with people who know people in that situation. I also understand it's hard letting yourself be vulnerable in this way. I think that anyone with an ounce of humanity who sees this will find their respect for you rising. But even knowing that, it doesn't make it an easy decision. I do hope, though, that you'll be willing to do this. I think it will be a real gift to all of us.

As I considered, I reached out to my friend and faculty colleague, Jennifer Aaker, for advice. She's a well-regarded expert on meaning, purpose, and the power of story, and the author of *The Dragonfly Effect: Quick, Effective, and Powerful Ways to Use Social Media to Drive Change*. She not only knew the power of story and its ripple effects in social media, but also understood how such a step might impact my role in the institution and reappointment in particular. She said, "JD, you don't need to worry about the impact of a TED talk within the school. But are you sure you are ready for the attention you might face going so public with this? It could become quite intense."

I took about another month to decide. During that time I lost another friend to suicide—someone with whom I'd attended school from childhood and graduated high school. If the intent of my talk was to "break the silence," then it felt like posting a talk on TED was a pretty powerful way to do that. Together with the team at TED we chose June 11, 2011, as the date to launch. This marked the eighth anniversary of my suicide attempt and brought light to a day that had previously held shame and darkness. TED's support in this effort was incredible; they had extra staff online that weekend and went to great lengths to be sure that if viewers were triggered by the talk, they could be directed to the right resources to get help.

To date my TED talk has over 1.8 million views and has been translated into 39 languages. Many of my students did indeed see it, but I never had to deal with any negative repercussions in or beyond the classroom because of my choice to be vulnerable and transparent. I was reappointed (twice) at the GSB and now hold a senior leadership role at Stanford's Knight-Hennessy Scholars program. It all worked out. I've even started working on my next book dedicated just to this subject. My working title is *The Bridge Back to Life: How One Man Came from the Edge of Death to the Center of Life*.

■ ■ ■

My own lived experience sourced my five tips in this section, from checking my motives, seeking the counsel of my husband and advisors, to preparing for the consequences. Over the years, when others come to me and say, "JD, I just don't know that I can share this," I respond much as Chris Anderson did when I was making my decision: If you're not sure, you may not yet be ready. Check your motives and know why you are disclosing before you attempt to take action. But if you do, be sure you're not doing it for your own self-motivated reasons. Disclose personally for the benefit of others.

5 Tailoring Your Communication to Your Setting

Just as you'll think carefully about your specific audience before crafting your communication, you should also think carefully about the setting in which you'll operate. Your communication strategy will be very different if you are presenting on the TED stage than if you are leading a team meeting. In this chapter, we'll lead you through some considerations to set you up for success in meetings both in-person and virtual, when on the stage, when co-presenting, when fielding questions, and when using slides.

Meetings

To really make a meeting successful, what you do before and afterward is crucial. Many times, the real work will occur before you ever set foot in the conference room. Or the real impact may occur in the meeting that happens *after* the meeting. The logistics of the meeting, though they may seem secondary, do matter.

Before you even send out the invitation for the meeting, think about who needs to be there. Is everyone essential? Jeff Bezos once said that the ideal team size for a meeting is a "two-pizza team." If the group can't be fed with two pizzas, it's too big. (Of course, you can't account for big appetites, or these days, if any of your colleagues are gluten-free. But we do what we can.)

Next, choose the location and the medium for the meeting. Will everyone be there in person? Will everyone be remote? Or—the most difficult but the most common situation—will the participants be joining from a number of locations? If you can bring everyone together in one place, do that. Tone will be easier to read, flow will be faster, and you won't have to deal with the vagaries of technology. But if you can't do that, you can and should still have a clear agenda and intent for your meeting. See Kara's sidebar for some information on this crucial step.

A Note from Kara: "Lead with Intent"

When we prepare content for a meeting, most of us think about what's going to happen when we're there: what we'll talk about, the points we'll cover, and who might speak. For example: *I'm going to cover our budgetary concerns, allow Juliana and Roma to speak, and solicit feedback on last week's pitch.* That's our agenda, and setting an agenda is certainly important. But if we leave our preparation there, we're missing a key step. We're missing our intent.

Think of your intent as your hoped-for outcomes of a meeting, conversation, or event. If your agenda is what's going to happen, your intent is what will result from your agenda. In other words, your agenda is a means to an end goal. By the end of your meeting, what actions do you want people to take? How do you want them to feel? What do you want them to understand?

Articulating your intent to yourself is a crucial step in identifying the content you want to share. It helps you decide what content will contribute to your goals. If you are able to share your intent at the beginning of your meeting, you will be more likely to drive toward that outcome, minimize miscommunication around why you're forwarding your agenda, and stay on track.

Once you're in the meeting, stick to the guidelines you've set for yourself. If you're leading the meeting, get there early. Start on time, and end on time. (Yes, it should go without saying. But if you've ever attended a meeting—anywhere! with anyone!—you know why we're mentioning it now.) As Kara mentioned above, you should state your intent clearly and early, and do your best to follow the agenda that serves your intent.

If you're presenting during the meeting or offering slides, be thoughtful about how to interact with the slides, position yourself in the room, and distribute materials. If you're working from a printed deck, make sure it corresponds to the deck your audience will see (with the same page numbers). Make as few extra notes as possible so that you don't appear overly reliant on them. This will help you connect with the group in front of you. One of my colleagues shared that she gave one of the best presentations of her life when she forgot her own deck. She had more of a conversation with the others present when she wasn't bound to a script. But of course, to minimize the chance you'll have a technical problem, always bring a copy of your deck with you on a USB drive or email it to yourself before you arrive.

Make your deck easy for your audience to follow by guiding them directly to each slide. Use highlights or sticky notes to emphasize important sections. Or try purposely leaving a section blank that you'd like the audience to fill in. My first sales job was in grad school, selling advertising on a desk blotter that was given to college students. My mentor showed me that if I provided a "mini mockup" of the calendar and quoted the prices to prospective advertisers, most of them would write down the prices as I spoke. When they later looked back at the document and saw their own handwriting, it formed a more lasting impression.

Since every member of your meeting will typically have a copy of your deck, I try to bring something that everyone will look at together for at least a portion of the presentation. One group of executives I trained from Rabobank in the Netherlands had to deliver an update to senior leaders on their three-week fact-finding trip in California. Rather than offer a small map of the state in each person's deck, they instead unfolded a large AAA map in the middle of the conference table and marked it up as they went through the conversation, showing the various stops on their trip. My clients who work in architecture or real estate development often bring a floor plan and several sheets of clear acetate when reviewing building or site plans, so the decision-makers can sketch what they hope to see in the next iteration.

Non-verbal communication experts agree that if you can stand while others remain seated, you gain some power. So decide whether you can stand to deliver the more formal part of your presentation or meeting agenda, then sit to field questions or facilitate conversation. If this feels too awkward or out-of-the-norm, consider standing for just a few moments. Perhaps stand to illustrate something on the whiteboard or flipchart, then remain on your feet a bit longer as you facilitate some comments about what you've just illustrated.

Where you sit in your meeting should not be accidental. If you are the primary presenter, take a position beside or at a corner adjacent to the decision-maker. Research by Mark Knapp at the University of Vermont shows that if you share a corner or side of the table with the decision-maker, it will be easier to reach an agreement. Conversely, the most adversarial position is directly opposite someone. (Just think of a chess game.) Try to sit where you can maximize eye contact. Sitting near the end of a table in a long board room lets you easily see most of the people in the room (and avoids the "tennis match" position where you must turn your head every time someone speaks from a different end of the table). Choose a seat that minimizes the barriers between you and your audience. In a room where you regularly meet or present, you may already know which seat provides you the greatest non-verbal advantage; in an unfamiliar space, you'll have to quickly decide which is the best option. When you are on a team for a presentation, allow the person with the greatest speaking role to enter the room and choose a seat first.

If you're thinking about distributing a pitch deck, delay that as long as possible. Take some time to share your intent and agenda, and talk about the audience's goals for the meeting before you begin. Once they have their decks, you will be competing for their attention. Your initial read of the audience can help you guide them to the material that will interest them most.

As a facilitator, you'll also want to think about how to balance the voices in the room. Too often, meetings become the domain of extroverts. Look for opportunities to include voices that aren't as forthcoming. You might build something into your meeting that allows participants to reflect quietly, to go to the whiteboard to offer ideas, or to provide information in writing. Those who aren't speaking might have great value to add. Think about how you can bring them into the conversation in a way that doesn't put them on the spot, but honors their contributions.

A Note from Kara: "A Few Words on Interruption"

At the risk of interrupting this chapter too much, let's take a moment to discuss that persistent bugbear of meetings: interruption. My clients often ask me how to interrupt or get their voices into the room, as well as how to prevent others from interrupting. As long as you're operating respectfully, here are few best practices you might try:

- **Vocal:** From the moment you send your voice into the room, make sure your tone is strong, your volume is "normal" (neither hesitantly quiet nor boorishly loud), and you're starting with the first words of your sentence rather than a filler word or an intro phrase. Content will grab others' attention more effectively than fillers will—and that goes for your vocal tone as well as the words you use. You can also use a frame to signal how much information you plan to share. If you have two points, say so up front. If interruption has been a particular problem in your group, you can also signal "intent to finish" up front with a phrase like, "I want to make sure I finish two points before we move on in the conversation."

- **Physical:** Signal readiness to speak with movement. I recommend that my clients move slightly closer or further from the table to draw others' eyes and give them an opening to speak. As we'll discuss in our upcoming conversation about virtual meetings, if you're dialing in remotely, you can tap the computer with your pen to bring the video focus back to you and create the same effect.

Virtual Meetings

Virtual meetings come with their own unique set of challenges and opportunities. On the plus side, virtual meetings make last-minute communication possible, are a low-cost alternative to pricey travel, and can allow you to include leaders who would otherwise not be able to collaborate with you. I was only able to invite Michael Rezendes, the Pulitzer Prize–winning *Boston Globe* reporter who broke the Catholic church scandal, to speak to my class about his experience because a virtual option was available. I couldn't have afforded to fly him out to Palo Alto, but we were able to find the time to have a call that offered my students valuable access to a new perspective. And technology continues to get better and better—what's possible now simply wasn't possible 15 or even five years ago. More and more, meeting virtually offers many of the benefits of being there.

But of course, meeting over video or phone call doesn't offer *all* the benefits of being there. Technology, while always progressing, can sink you if you're having connection, audio, or video problems. People tend to be less interactive virtually, so it's harder to gauge the tone of the group and how they're feeling. Time zone differences can make virtual meetings hard to schedule. But a few best practices can put you in a good position to maximize the opportunities of this medium and minimize the inconveniences.

Suggest that your audio calls be conducted over video. This will give you the all-important advantage of some visual connection with your colleagues and make you feel more present. I often remember the story of one of my students who was preparing to interview for admission to the GSB. In preparation, he bought a new suit, booked a plane ticket, and readied himself for an in-person conversation. But the day of the flight, it snowed heavily and he was unable to travel. His in-person meeting was rescheduled as an audio call. Nonetheless, on the morning of the call he got up, showered, and put on that new suit as though he were meeting in person or over video. He did everything he could to make himself feel like he was there. And probably needless to say, he got in.

If you can't create a video opportunity, add as much dynamism as you can into your experience of an audio call. Use a headset rather than speaker phone, and walk around your room. Gesture as you would in person. Focus on vocal variety, energy, and confidence. You'll need to compensate for the lack of these visual cues with your voice and your word choice.

If you'll be sharing slides during your call, expect that they'll mutate in the act of sending. Simple slides will travel better and need less clarification, so make sure that you pare down anything that's text-heavy or data-heavy. Check any links ahead of time to make sure they work. It's much harder to course-correct for technological differences when you have neither in-person rapport nor visual cues to aid you.

If you're lucky enough to be able to connect over video, pay attention to how you're framed in the picture. Make eye contact with the camera and make sure you are not backlit. I keep a special light behind my computer monitor to light me properly during these calls, but if you don't have one, even the white light from your computer monitor will work.

To keep your video calls effective and engaging, you'll want to focus on keeping them lively. I like to make a drawing of a clock face at the beginning of the meeting. As each person enters, I draw a line on the clock so that I can keep track of the order in which people joined (Figure 5.1). As people speak, I make a tick mark next to their names so that I can keep track of who's contributing. That way, it's easy to see who I should try to include more, or call on in a quieter moment. Sometimes I'll ask all participants to summarize their reactions to our conversation in "just three words." This technique encourages everyone to speak, but it keeps things brief and resets the collaborative atmosphere.

Consider offering breakout groups on a longer call. Zoom makes this particularly easy: I can divide people into groups for a few minutes, then bring them back. But you can also try this over any free video conferencing service. Set up different call-in numbers for each

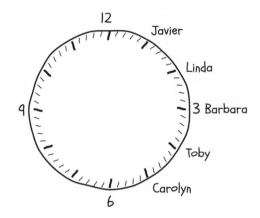

Figure 5.1 Clock for virtual meetings, with hashtags to indicate when participants have spoken

of your breakout groups. When it's time to break for smaller discussions, assign those numbers to participants, give each group a topic for discussion, and instruct them to call back in to the primary meeting number at a specific time.

On Stage (TED Talks, LOWKeynotes, and the Like)

Without question, TED has changed the game for what's expected of presentations. I can still remember February 2009, when a student asked me if I knew of TED. My response was, "Ted who?" By the next year, February 2010, I was attending my first TED conference, and in February 2011, I delivered my first TED talk. (You might say I quickly got to know who TED was!) My evolution of familiarity with the TED organization matches the rise of TED on a global scale. When I started using TED talk clips in my teaching, maybe 5 percent of the audience would know the reference. Now, maybe 5 percent of the audience *doesn't* know what TED is. More than any other single medium or event, the rise of TED talks and the TED style of speaking has changed product launches, keynotes—even graduation speeches. Quite often I find that event planners will say, "We want the ambiance to feel like we're at TED" or "We're looking for a TED-style talk" as a shorthand for the intimate, passion-driven, story-rich genre. While there are certainly those who worry that we're "dumbing down" big ideas when we slot them into 12- or 18-minute segments, I think the rise of TED has been much more of a gift than a curse for our global community.

Following in TED's footsteps, we realized that at the GSB, students had abundant opportunities to speak, but nothing that represented a high-stakes leadership presentation. So in the fall of 2011, we sought to do just that—and the LOWKeynotes program was born. At the GSB, our motto is "Change lives. Change organizations. Change the world." From "lives, organization, world" we borrowed the LOW to characterize these unique keynotes, in which students talk about the impact they wish to make within a topic they're passionate about.

As we're deciding who to accept into the program, we look at two key metrics: the strength of the topic or content, and the skill of the presenter. Of course many candidates earn high marks in both areas. But more often, as a coaching unit we're helping students to move toward mastery in one of these areas.

To succeed in an onstage setting, work first has to be done on the content, the idea itself. Only after the idea, the argument, the stories, and their supports are crystallized should you focus on delivery. We recommend dividing your lead time in half and spending the first half on content, then the second half on delivery. So if you have four weeks to prepare for your keynote, try to have your content locked two weeks out from the event so that you can really focus on your delivery to make it shine.

When it comes time for delivery, we encourage students to familiarize themselves with the space in which they'll be presenting. The stakes are higher for this sort of a presentation, so don't let your environment be the factor that derails you—particularly when you can do the work to make it familiar ahead of time. We urge students to practice their LOWKeynotes in the event spaces and to consider how they'll use the stage to their advantage. When will they move? How much larger and bolder will their gestures need to be so that they don't get lost on stage? We ask them to think about their visuals: how many they'll be using, how much they may have to compete with their visuals, and where their visuals will appear. Even what you wear matters: For many years, students always presented in front of a background of whiteboard in a large stadium-seating classroom; if they wore a white top, they would show up as floating heads on the video. Think about wearing something in which you feel confident and mobile; it should not only be appropriate to your topic and your audience (for example, you likely wouldn't wear a tuxedo to a talk in casual Silicon Valley!), but it should also take your environment into account.

Few of us begin our onstage journeys as expert content developers *and* experts at delivery. But focusing on idea first, yet leaving enough time to hone delivery, usually nets impactful results.

When Co-Presenting

If presenting on your own is a balancing act, presenting with teammates might be a feat of balance with a little juggling thrown in for good measure. Not only will you need to focus on your verbal, vocal, and visual, but you'll also need to be intentional about how you weave your part of the presentation with those of your teammates.

Bookend Your Strongest Speakers

Because you never get that second chance to make a strong first or last impression, position your strongest speakers in the opening and closing positions. This won't mean that the speakers in the middle of your presentation are off the hook; in fact, those presenters will be challenged to hold the audience's attention at the moments when engagement often wanes. Those who speak second, third, and fourth will end up being specialists, addressing the details of the proposal. The opener and closer will be generalists. So if you have people on your team with specialized knowledge, perhaps the best role for them is to speak in the middle of your presentation.

Choreograph Smooth, Audience-Focused Transitions

Imagine the join between two carriages of a train. The join is held together with a pin, connecting each carriage to the next. You might think of your transitional content the same way: it should connect the content that came before to the content that comes next. One speaker may pose a question that the next speaker answers. One may do a cost analysis; the person who speaks next may begin with, "Cost is central to our decision, as is revenue"—and then begin a discussion of revenue.

You've no doubt seen the same common transition pitfalls that we have:

1. The anchorman handoff:

   JD: "And now, Kara will talk to you about pricing."

   Kara: "Thanks, JD. Let me talk to you all about pricing."

2. Repeating the exact same thing that's just been said.

3. No transition whatsoever. JD stops speaking and sits; Kara stands and starts speaking—like ships in the night.

Instead of these options, encourage each speaker to remain in place until the next teammate has taken the stage. Someone should always be in charge of the stage. Person B should walk up and claim the stage before Person A walks off. Person B may even start talking while walking, then finish in front of Person A. The new speaker should be closest to the audience, and the old speaker should exit from behind the colleague who is taking over.

The Cue-to-Cue Rehearsal

If a team feels truly solid about what all members will say and where they will begin and end, they can practice using what theater professionals call the cue-to-cue rehearsal. Person A can deliver the first and last lines, and then Person B will do the same, continuing onward until everyone has participated. In just 30 to 60 seconds, your whole team can do a run-through that reinforces your sense of cohesion and clarity.

When Fielding Questions

In the mid-1990s I volunteered for SpeakOUT Boston, a speakers bureau that provided LGBT (now LGBTQIAA) speakers on a wide variety of topics, mainly focused on conducting educational programs about LGBTQIAA issues, sharing our lives, and educating our communities about issues that divide all of us. Our classic "Q-and-A panel for an hour" began with about 45 minutes of us talking, followed by 15 minutes of the audience asking questions. Over time we found that participants evaluated our events more positively (and frankly were more fun) when we reduced the amount of prepared content and increased the time for questions. We went from a ratio of 45/15 minutes spent on speaking to Q-and-A, to 30/30, to 15/45, and the audiences seemed to like it more and more. Once, I recall, we even did 5/55, which was essentially "ask me anything"—and it was a hit.

Long before I started teaching leadership communication, this experience taught me that questions matter. They *really* matter. We should not fear questions at the end of a presentation (or for the very bravest souls among us, within a presentation). In fact, we should welcome questions. When our audience asks us questions, it means we've inspired them enough to engage, inquire, take a risk, and speak their minds.

Yet time after time I've seen individuals and teams fall apart during the question portion of a presentation. The lessons on questions that I share with leaders fall into two broad areas:

- *The basics:* making time, setting up, visuals awareness, and restating

- *Reframing techniques:* taking on the listener's perspective when fielding particularly challenging questions

Making Time, Setting Up, Visuals Awareness, and Restating

Let's begin with the basics. Leave time for questions. That's it. Don't tell us you will take questions at the end, and then run out of time to do so. Leave time for questions.

In team presentations in particular, I consider Q-and-A to be simply the "next speaker" from the team. Try to preempt applause and set up the questions directly. It's often best to synthesize your main message once more, then segue into the question portion, rather than ending and asking, "Any questions?" To do that is a bit like putting a car in park at 60 mph. Instead, use the momentum of your presentation to guide you smoothly into the question section of your presentation.

If you are using slides, consider carefully what image you want projected during Q-and-A. Often this slide will be up longer than any other slide in your deck, so make it matter. If you don't have a slide that meets this criterion, you may choose to bring up a blank slide and take questions with no projected images.

Finally, try your best to get in the habit of restating the questions. You can do this simply by changing the question into a statement. "When did you finish the project?" becomes not simply "1997," but "We finished the project in 1997." While this may seem like a simple phrasing choice, restating reassures your audience that you truly heard the question and provides a memorable sound bite for those who may not have heard the original questioner. Especially if you are speaking to the press, offering a clear, concise sound bite with the proper context attached will ensure that your audience receives your answer in the way you intended to frame it.

Reframing Techniques: Taking on the Listener's Perspective When Fielding Particularly Challenging Questions

At a more advanced level, there will be many times when you need to listen carefully to the question and reframe it before answering. Our colleague Stephanie Soler helped us to better understand this perspective with the helpful image shown in Figure 5.2.

Stephanie suggests that there are three essential steps when we are responding to a question within a meeting or presentation. Each step corresponds to a mindset that leaders may find helpful to adopt. First, a leader must listen not simply to hear the question, but to listen deeply with a mindset of curiosity. It's so easy to hear how a question begins and start formulating an answer, but do your best to avoid that bad habit. Instead, strive to listen actively. This may involve some of

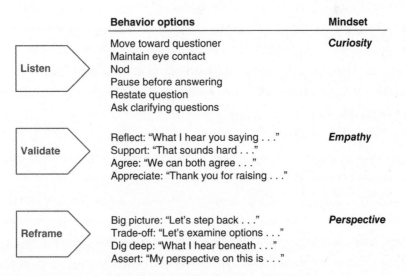

Figure 5.2 Essentials of responding to a question

the behaviors listed in Figure 5.2, such as nodding, moving toward the questioner, and simply restating the question. It may help at this point to ask a clarifying question, again keeping yourself curious and not defensive.

Once you are clear on the question being asked, you may move to validating the question with a mindset of empathy. You want to relate to and connect with the person who asked the question. This is easy when that person is confused by a complex topic you presented, but difficult when the person is directly challenging your position. Nonetheless, don't skip this step. You need not engage all of the behaviors listed above, but try to employ at least one to validate the person who asked the question. "I can see why you might think that" or "I used to see it that way too, but I've found . . ." are examples of ways you might validate a question you receive.

At this point you might simply be able to answer the question, but occasionally you will need to reframe the question before you answer. In doing so, try to adopt the mindset of perspective rather than animosity. If you've demonstrated that you listened to and validated the question, it should be easier to then offer a different perspective. I try to avoid directly saying, "I don't buy the premise of your question." Instead I prefer to say something softer and more connected like, "I see the heart of the question differently." This three-step process and its corollary mindsets have offered leaders a simple way to respond with less confrontation and greater connection to their audiences.

While I tend to shy away from political examples, particularly on charged topics, there is one vivid example I often share at this point in my classes. In 2000, Hillary Clinton was running for U.S. Senate in New York. After Rudy Giuliani dropped out of the race due to health reasons, Clinton faced Rick Lazio, a congressman representing New York's second district. While she was a pro-choice Democrat, Lazio was a pro-life Republican. It was inevitable that questions about this discrepancy would arise in their televised debate. When those questions arose, rather than immediately jump into a contentious fray, Mrs. Clinton began by emphasizing that there was one thing both candidates could agree on: neither of them wanted to see more abortions. She then went on to reframe the question further by noting that when the economy does well, fewer women seek abortions. She effectively moved the discussion from a hostile party-line argument between pro-life and pro-choice positions to a discourse on economic development and job creation. Her position about a woman's right to choose remained unchanged, but she took the question back to its premise and reframed it to a place where she wanted the discussion to go.

If you're interested in more on this topic, I always guide leaders to Jerry Weisman's 2005 book, *In the Line of Fire* (Pearson) for more detail. Here Weisman, a pioneer of Silicon Valley communication coaching, provides multiple frameworks and examples of great strategies for answering tough questions.

When Using Slides

Let me begin this section by acknowledging what we've chosen not to cover in this book on leadership communication: how to design slides effectively. This is a *huge* topic better left to the experts in the field of visual communication. I urge you to explore *Slide:ology* by Nancy Duarte and *Storytelling with Data* by Cole Nussbaumer Knaflic, two "best in class" books on the subject. In this section, we will briefly cover some basic tips on slide design as well as strategies for effectively integrating your presentation delivery with slides behind you.

First and foremost, I urge you to remember: your slides are not your presentation! In my very first year of teaching back at NYU, I recall a student who came in to my office hours upset with her presentation grade. She waved her slide deck at me, describing how great it was and why it deserved a higher grade. I acknowledged she had earned a 5/5 on the slides, but the slides were *not* the presentation. They were but one *element* of her presentation. After she calmed down a bit, we had a more nuanced conversation about delivery, content, audience interaction, handling questions, and so much more. Those elements were the heart of her communication with the audience, and it was there that she needed to focus more of her attention. She had fallen into the common trap of thinking the slides were the presentation.

We often tell students, "The night before a major presentation, you are better off getting one more hour of sleep than spending one more hour revising your slides." While I resist the constraint as a presenter, I see the value when conferences require speakers to "lock and submit their slides" days or even weeks before the scheduled talk. I've not resorted to this in my classes yet, but may do so soon. This choice allows the final hours and days to be focused on delivery, not content—as it should be.

When I do teach slide design to leaders, I emphasize these five general points about slides:

1. **KISS: Keep It Simple, Stanford.** I often point to Apple's packaging and ads as the aspirational standard here. Apple uses white space so effectively and reduces clutter remarkably well. Taking an "Apple eye" to slides can help reduce any unnecessary items. Cole calls this "reducing cognitive load on your audience."

2. **Deliver Only One Message Per Slide.** As a complement to keeping your visuals simple, be sure to cover one and only one message per slide. Break complex messages into a series of slides to ensure that each message doesn't have competition.

3. **Begin Headlines with Power Verbs.** The most important real estate on a slide is the heading; make it matter. Your heading is typically your best place to communicate your message to your audience. To create an active and engaging presentation, use the power verb list provided in Appendix A on your slides.

4. **Include Animations Strategically.** When leading a conversation your audience, it may help you to reveal some information line by line. Do avoid going crazy with all the choices PowerPoint and Keynote offer (who really needs a line of text to spin and grow in front of us?), but don't shy away from purposeful and thoughtful animations on your slides.

5. **Select Your Q-and-A Slide with Care.** Your Q-and-A slide may well be up longer than any other slide in your deck. Repeat a killer chart or image from earlier in the talk, or simply restate your thesis with your contact information. If you don't have a strong image for your Q-and-A, then choose a blank slide. Do not place a huge question mark on the screen; standing below that slide simply makes you look clueless—not the impact you want to have with your audience!

When you are delivering a talk with projected slides, you'll want to think about a few best practices that will allow you to present smoothly:

1. **Announce Before You Advance.** Maintain the lead role; tell your audience what slide is coming as you bring that slide into view. You want to be driving the slides, not having them drive you.

2. **Learn the Shortcuts.** All of the platforms for slide creation contain some simple shortcuts. For example, hitting the "B" key on your keyboard will take the screen to black or "W" will take it to white. Pressing the key a second time will return you directly to the slide you were projecting. Hitting the number of the slide you wish to move to, followed by "enter," will take you there. (I once got applause from an audience at a workshop for this simple trick!)

3. **Eliminate Laser Pointers (unless you are presenting to a group of cats).** Even though your remote may offer you the power of shining a bright red laser onto your screen, don't take the bait.

In a small room, simply walk to the screen, touch the image you want to emphasize, turn back to the audience, and talk about the element. In a larger space or with multiple screens, use color or shading to emphasize the element, not your laser pointer.

We're limiting ourselves to this brief treatment of slide use in leadership presentations because we urge you to learn more from those who specialize in this area. For a more expansive discussion of the topic, check out my website and the books indicated earlier in this chapter.

6 Tailoring Your Communication to Your Identity

Our personal identities are not just an accessory to our communication; they inform our unique perspectives, leadership styles, and goals. We may perceive elements of our identities that we don't think twice about when communicating as leaders (for example, my well-known love of caffeine rarely comes up), but often we will need to reconcile core elements of who we are with best practices for how to communicate the ideas that matter to us.

In this chapter, we cover some special topics that arise when you are leading in your non-native language, when you are an LGBTQ leader, when you are a woman or female-identifying leader, a veteran, or a rookie leader. We urge you to review these sections even if you don't consider yourself a member of these groups. You may find that some of the best practices we offer will serve your communication, but more importantly, we hope they will broaden your perspective on the communication challenges that your colleagues, mentees, and direct reports might face. Our identities exist in constant conversation with our environments, so as always, use these suggestions as a starting point for how to navigate your personal identity within the context where you lead.

Leading in Your Second (or Third, or Fourth) Language

In our increasingly global world, many of us may find ourselves presenting, speaking, negotiating, writing, studying, or working in a language that is not our native tongue. When you are leading in a language that is not your own, it's important to remember that *except where it impedes clarity*, your identity—your accent, your traditions, your values—are central to the leadership you offer. When students ask me if they should try to reduce or change their accents, I unequivocally answer no. Your accent tells part of your story. It informs the path you took to arrive at your current leadership moment. And it offers useful context to your peers. Claim your international identity and own it proudly.

The only reason you might want to approach your leadership differently than a native speaker is if others have difficulty understanding your ideas. Clarity is key—be sure you can be understood in the dominant language of the group.

If you are writing, seek out a coach who can encourage you to clarify unwieldy word choices or awkward constructions. A copy editor—someone who simply corrects your work—will not be as helpful to your progress as a coach who corrects the first paragraph of your piece, then lets you correct the second. Seek to understand *why* corrections are offered, and with repeated practice, you'll be able to write more clearly without the assistance of a coach.

Sometimes while presenting, you might find that adding a few extra words to your slides can clarify a word that's hard for you to pronounce. For example, if you know it's difficult for you to pronounce "flamingo," you might consider adding an image of a flamingo or simply the written word to aid your audience's comprehension.

A Note from Kara: "Slow Down Your Speech to Speed Up Comprehension"

While speaking, the biggest favor you can offer yourself and your audience is to slow down. I offer this advice to leaders who communicate in their native language as well as to those who don't. Slowing down your speech not only allows you better control of your content, helping you to be more concise and intentional, but it also helps you to enunciate better so that audiences can understand every word.

To practice, try speaking a sentence aloud with exaggerated slowness. See whether you can close your mouth between words. It may sound like, "We. Suggest. Increased. Personnel. On. This. Project." I know: It's incredibly awkward. But this exaggeration of articulating each word helps build the muscle memory around speaking more slowly. When you speed up to a conversational pace, cue yourself with the word "slow." By practicing with exceptional slowness, your new slow pace may not feel quite as uncomfortable.

With practice, you'll find that slowing down your speech will help you minimize filler words, choose your language more carefully, and elevate your leadership presence—no matter what language you speak.

Leading as an LGBTQ Person

In 2016 two of my colleagues, Sarah Soule and Tom Wurster, launched a bold new executive program, the first of its kind: a week-long summer institute for LGBTQ leaders. This straight tenured ally and gay former Boston Consulting Group managing director did more to change the

dialogue about LGBTQ leaders at Stanford (and beyond) than any
other single program or effort to date. Their vision was clear: to provide
support and education for senior leaders aspiring to be in the C suite,
but not yet there. As of 2019 only three publicly traded firms are led
by out LGBTQ leaders: Tim Cook at Apple, Jim Fitterling at Dow,
and Beth Ford at Land O'Lakes. We truly have a great need to change
the pipeline.

A Note on Labels

I will often use the acronym LGBTQ for "Lesbian, Gay, Bisexual, Transgender, Queer"; but sometimes for variety I may simply say "gay." I struggle with label usage here, as I am a fierce
advocate for inclusion and know that "LGBTQ" falls short
for some with identities beyond those five letters. Yet I am an
equally fierce advocate for clear and concise writing. I'm trying
to balance both here. Those who are even more "woke" than
I am include "+" at the end to include an even wider audience,
but I've not yet adopted this particular convention.

Sarah and Tom invited me to be a part of the inaugural faculty
group and have continued to invite me back each year. Through
this work with hundreds of remarkable executives from across
the globe, I was able to craft and polish the model that follows in
this section. Each year it changes a bit more, but I'm delighted
with what has evolved and have shared it with both gay and ally
leaders at a wide range of firms, including Amgen, Bloomberg,
Bristol-Meyers Squib, and Google, as well as non-profits like
Columbia University, Out & Equal, Reaching Out MBA, and the
Victory Fund.

Many leaders not in the LGBTQ community have remarked that the model I'm about to share doesn't just apply to the LGBTQ community, but to all of us. While I concur, I continue to teach this model specifically to the LGBTQ leaders I serve, using unique examples from that community. As a gay man myself, I entered and matured in the workforce with few mentors and role models to guide me. That is why those resources I did have stood out to me as particularly valuable. In the early 1990s, I worked at three different educational firms for Mark Mishkind, who was my first out gay mentor. He offered me more than I think he knows about the challenge of leading in spite of marginalization. A full 15 years later in 2007, when I was hired at the GSB, I was still the first out gay faculty member the school had ever appointed. I did learn later an out lesbian had retired that spring, but for many years, we two were the sum total of the GSB's out LGBTQ hires. While younger leaders today have many more examples to rely upon than I had, marginalization still exists, particularly when we look at this personal identity on a global scale. That is why providing resources that speak to this community continues to be crucial.

Begin with a blank white canvas. For me this represents authenticity. I strongly urge all gay leaders to decide for themselves what is authentic. Some are closeted at work and out in other parts of their lives; some are introverts, others extroverts; some are more discreet while others, like me, bring up my husband and kids when appropriate in a business context (like right here!). But leaders must do the important "inside job" of deciding who they are and what aspects of their gender identity and sexual orientation they wish to share with their world at work. While I am a huge advocate, on a cultural and corporate level, that we should all be "out and proud," on an individual level I recognize that this choice is highly personal. No one can force a choice of expression on another. We all must come to our own decision of what works for us and what is authentic for us.

And while I have amassed a large number of communication examples from leaders in the gay community, I also think we lose our individuality if we try to present exactly like Frances Frei or Megan Rapinoe or Pete Buttigieg or Maeve DuVally or any of the tens of thousands of other out LGBTQ leaders I could name. We must all be our own authentic selves first and foremost. Against this canvas of authenticity, however, I see four distinctions that can help leaders expand their presence as someone who happens to be LGBT and/ or Q. On top of this blank canvas I illustrate the LGBTQ Leadership Presence Radar, which contains four points: Confidence, Competence, Connection, and Clarity (Figure 6.1). Each of these four dimensions provides unique challenges and opportunities for leaders like me. While a perfect lavender diamond is aspirational (like mastery, perfection never comes), it points a direction for leaders to pursue.

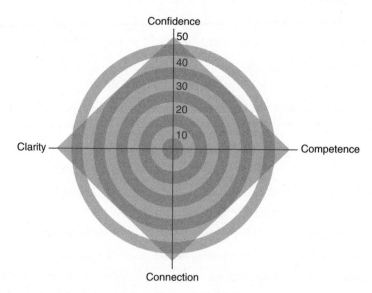

Figure 6.1 Lavender diamond of LGBTQ presence

(*Side note:* Over time, "LGBTQ Leadership Presence Radar" became too much of a mouthful to say (or remember) so now

I simply call this the Lavender Diamond framework or "The 4 C's." The original illustration of this framework was inspired by the work of Daniel Diermeier in his stellar book *Reputation Rules*. He created the Trust Radar for crisis communication, which had the elements of empathy, transparency, expertise, and commitment. The greater leaders score on these four points, the greater trust they build with the community. I encourage you to read his book, particularly if looking at the art of communication and management in a crisis.)

Confidence: Stepping into Your Power as a Leader

We've already covered much of this concept earlier in our book, but it's a different issue for those who don't identify as straight. Many of us have for years heard negative messages about our being gay or coming out. Whether overt or subtle, almost every gay person I know has experienced some level of homophobia, heterosexism, or (at its worst) outright discrimination or violence. Often, this comes at the hands of family members or religious leaders whom we may cherish and respect. This can result in an experience of internalized homophobia (defined as the involuntary belief by members of the gay community that the homophobic lies, stereotypes, and myths about them are true). When we have a strong interior voice saying, "You aren't good enough," it's really challenging to step past that and put yourself out in the world as a leader, even if you're not discussing issues related to your sexual orientation or gender expression. So the first step for many in our community is to "go within before going out" and be clear about our choices and intentions in communication. This doesn't require counseling or therapy (though that has massively helped me), but it does likely involve conversations with others. Relying on a mentor you respect or your significant other can empower you to be ready to share powerfully from this place.

Once this step is complete, I point people to the guidance and resources covered in our earlier chapter on anxiety management.

As we discussed in our earlier conversation about anxiety management, I do find that striking expansive power poses and reframing the thought "I am anxious" to "I am excited" are two of the most powerful and actionable elements to consider.

Finally, I challenge leaders to consider: "If not you, who?" It may be uncomfortable to be the first openly trans leader in a firm or industry, but somebody must go first. And, by going first, we honor our LGBTQ ancestors who came before us and may inspire the younger generation to go even further. Each year I get to address the NextGen Leaders group (https://leadnextgen.org/), which brings together a diverse and inspiring group of LGBTQ leaders under 30 to help hone their leadership skills. I remind them that they stand on the shoulders of greatness. Were it not for Bayard Rustin, Maggie Stumpp, Audrey Lourde, Harvey Milk, and others, we would not enjoy the rights and privileges we have won. We owe it to them to make the most of the rich opportunity we've been given.

Finally, it bears repeating: Anxiety is not just common . . . it's natural. Courageous leaders don't speak and write without fear, but in spite of it. Be bold. Be confident. Step up. Speak out.

Clarity: Removing Doubt and Ambiguity from Your Communication

Strong leaders deliver clear, unambiguous messages that we can easily recall. In 2018 Frances Frei broke decades of tradition at TED with her talk: She used a blackboard! She also provided a beautiful system for structuring messages with your main point first, diagrammed as a triangle. She recounted the story of her year-long sabbatical from Harvard Business School to take on the senior vice presidency for leadership and strategy at embattled rideshare company Uber. She wove the need for clarity and authenticity together beautifully. One iconic moment is when she guides leaders to make their points at the beginning of their remarks in a meeting; that way, if you get cut off, you will still get credit for having made the point.

It often takes more time to write and speak clearly. It requires drafts and revisions. It often involves getting tough feedback from others, then iterating based on that input. But by following the approaches we advocate throughout this book, you can make your points clear, memorable, and actionable. One such example is Erin Uritus's 2018 address to the entire Out and Equal Conference at their annual summit. With rich rhetoric, she was able to introduce herself, honor her predecessor, and call the audience to engage more deeply. This feat proved particularly challenging as a bisexual in the LGBTQ community; I've had some bisexual students say it feels like the LGTQ community.

Competence: Increasing Credibility Through Good Work and Good Prep

As we round the corners of the diamond, we come to competence. In my view, competence has two components. The first is communication competence (or mastery, if you will) in writing and speaking—the core subject of this book. If you struggle with writing skills or fear public speaking, it's crucial to advance yourself where you struggle. Seek out a coach, take a course, establish a peer relationship for accountability; do whatever it takes so that your competence as a communicator won't be questioned. When I read an email with typos in it, or hear a speaker using frequent filler words, I begin to question the credibility of the leader. Even as an educator I don't give room for "a good try" or people who have "gifts in other areas"; I wonder why nobody has proofed their work or coached their delivery. We all must communicate all the time; it's the one skill that translates across all fields and careers. We need to get this one right, particularly the higher we climb in an organization. Leaders experience scrutiny in so many ways. We do not need to hand our critics reasons to doubt us. Remember Kim Scott's story about Sheryl Sandberg's feedback on Kim's "um's" that we covered earlier. It's up to us to shore up the basics of leadership communication. You likely know this since you are reading this book, but it's important enough that it bears repeating.

But the second aspect of competence is even more crucial for LGBTQ leaders: being technically competent at our jobs. When we do good work, we increase our credibility more than any other action we can take. It's harder for me to provide clear tips and strategies on this point, because my readers will come from such diverse career fields. You will need to establish the expectations for your particular role, then ensure you can do these effectively. Again, the demand here is not for perfection, but competence. We all need to take on stretch assignments where we don't always know what's expected, but we likewise need to do our best to come up to speed quickly and leave no room for detractors to attack us. This is particularly crucial for those who are the first in a particular firm or career. I felt some of this when I came to Stanford as the first out gay member of the faculty in 2007.

The most vivid example of this that I can recall was from a panel at the December 2016 Victory Fund conference. This event, just weeks after the election of President Trump, was expected to be a celebration of sorts—but the outcome of the election changed all that. Conference organizers scrambled to revise the agenda so that it met the needs of our new reality as an LGBTQ community. One panel at the event was comprised of six ambassadors who had been appointed by President Obama. All six gay men knew they were going to be displaced on the day of Trump's inauguration. They shared powerful stories of what it was like to serve as out gay leaders in such high-profile positions, sometimes in countries where the culture did not embrace same-sex relationships. Two of the ambassadors, James Brewster (assigned to the Dominican Republic) and Ted Osius (assigned to Vietnam), spoke of being in the green room after their senate approval, but before being announced and sworn in. They both knew they were going to countries that would be unlikely to embrace (and more likely to oppose) them and their husbands.

Brewster shared with Osius, "We'd better do our jobs really, really well. All eyes will be on us." In that one statement he beautifully summarized what I mean by the necessity for competence in our profession. Leaders under scrutiny must be competent communicators, but also competent in their jobs. Leave no room for people to have justified cause to criticize; they will find enough unjustified reasons to do so!

Connection: Reaching Your Audience with Vulnerability and Storytelling

Admittedly that last section might feel a bit negative. As my friend and mentor Nancy Duarte says in her book *Illuminate*, we need to have both "encouraging" and "warning" communications to cause a difference in the world. So let's move from a rather "warning" component of the leadership presence radar to a more encouraging one: telling stories. The easiest tool to connect with your followers is to be a storyteller. Stories bridge the unfamiliar with the familiar; stories entertain, illuminate, and last. Years later my students can recall stories from my teaching more than the actual content or principles I taught. (As long as my stories were there to illustrate a point, I'm fine with that judgment by alumni.)

We've already dedicated some time to storytelling earlier in this section, so here I merely want to emphasize the value and power of authentic stories from our own unique perspective. It's not that as leaders we must tell our entire sordid coming-out story each time we address a group, but rather that we should feel as comfortable sharing stories about our lives, interests, and families just as our non-gay colleagues do. Let me offer two examples from my own life.

When teaching a workshop I will often weave in some elements of my own life. I will say something like, "My husband Ken and I adopted our oldest son from foster care when he was 16. Toby arrived in our home with an unrealistic expectation about what his dads were willing to fork out for sneakers." These are the opening few lines of a story I tell in my storytelling with data lesson; the relevance is that in his quest for sneakers, Toby shared a TED@IBM talk by Josh Luber with me that changed my view on the value of sneakers on the secondary market. The point I make in class is that Josh used a powerful illustration of data to close his talk, and Toby's reuse of that data on me was compelling. But by adding in that I have a husband and that we have kids through adoption, I connect with other parents in the audience while (perhaps) challenging their stereotypes of gay men. I come out by telling a story that's decidedly *not* about coming out.

Here's a second example from the spring of 2019. In addition to attending the church my husband pastors, I also attend my own church, a remarkable Roman Catholic parish in the heart of the Castro, Most Holy Redeemer. This year on the feast of Pentecost I hosted a group of Stanford MBA students from the school's Catholic Student Association. I love getting to share the joy and power of MHR with others, especially students who've never seen a gay-friendly Catholic parish. After communion I was standing behind the group of students and looking toward the priest at the altar. I realized that my group not only included several straight students with their young children, but some gay students at different places in their own coming-out processes. By my invitation, I was able to expose all of them to the rare experience of LGBTQ people of faith in a Catholic context. When I tell this story, I'm able to share not just the unexpected intersection of Catholicism and LGBTQ identity, but the commonality of simply "going to church on Sunday."

Admittedly it may be a bit easier for those of us with spouses and families to "come out with ease" in a talk or blog than it is for single leaders; but with clarity and creativity we can find ways to bring our full selves into our communication. I don't believe I "wear my gay identity" on my sleeve, but I also don't shy away from it. I grew up with a scarcity of role models. I want to do my part to be sure I'm exemplifying the challenges and rewards of my life fully for those with whom I write and speak.

Pulling It All Together: The Lavender Diamond

Over the years this model has evolved quite a bit; the terms shift, the order changes, and the examples are updated each time I teach it. In fact, I hesitated to include this section for fear it would be outdated between when I hit *submit* on the manuscript and when I held the first printed copy in my hands. But the lesson remains consistent: against a canvas of authenticity we all want to strive to be confident, clear, competent, and connected communicators. The challenges are great, but in my mind even greater for LGBTQ leaders. Yet the rewards for us leaders and those who follow us are worth the risk. Aspire to extend your own lavender diamond a little further each time you write or speak.

Leading as a Woman

Recently a team of students delivered a final presentation in my strategic communication class. The topic they chose to present was "Speech Starters." Ilana, a first-year student with generally excellent delivery skills, began in role-play mode, pretending to deliver a very poor opening. A peer, Sam, entered the role play by interrupting her after about 30 seconds: "Whoa, whoa, whoa, Ilana, stop. I need you to stop right there. That is not how you want to start a presentation. That was rough. The opener to a presentation is the most important part. Why don't you sit down, take a look, and we'll teach you the right way to start a presentation." Seven minutes later, after her peers had covered the content of designing a compelling opening, she returned and delivered a great opening (as expected). This "wrong way/interrupt/lesson/right way" construction is common for these final presentations and serves as a playful and easy way to get the class's attention, make some key points, and demonstrate the goal.

In fact, Ilana was the perfect foil for Sam's interruption. She is a strong student, and it was fun to see her "bomb on purpose" and be a bit more playful and informal.

But as I reviewed the feedback students gave, I realized an even greater lesson. Several women in the class questioned the need for "one more man to interrupt a woman at the GSB and explain how to do this right." I had not even considered that interpretation of what took place, but the feedback put into stark relief what so many female leaders face on a daily basis, and which often goes right past their well-meaning male colleagues (like me).

In the current era of #MeToo and #TimesUp, I am pleased that my students have a heightened sense of awareness about these situations, and am even more pleased that they brought it to me and their peers so we could all benefit from the dialogue. In this particular case it was not the intention of Ilana or Sam to be diminishing of her gifts and contribution. The presentation could just as easily featured Ilana interrupting Sam without impacting the content. But I'm glad they made the choice they did, because it allowed me to increase my awareness of some of the subtle and even unconscious bias around communication from a gender perspective. That lesson, for me, will stick much longer than their three steps to make your presentation opener more engaging.

Some readers may ask why I, a white, male baby-boomer academic, am writing on this topic. It's because I see the need in myself and others to approach communication mastery differently. I quickly acknowledge that I don't have the expertise here, but I do know where to find it. Until I began co-teaching with our colleague Allison Kluger, I never really considered the distinction of communicating differently as women or men. She urged me to add a session she would teach just for the women in our class on the topic. Over the years she had a few men request to take it, and she allowed it when there was a compelling reason like "I know I will lead women who will benefit from me knowing this" or "I want to be a better partner to my wife and better understand the challenges she faces."

One other co-teacher, Stephanie Soler, also engaged this topic during the quarters she taught at the GSB. I credit Stephanie with helping me to better understand this topic by sharing the strength and warmth continuum framework (Figure 6.2) from John Neffinger and Matthew Kohut's book *Compelling People*.

The authors argue that all of us operate with a mix of strength and warmth. As we become more skilled on each of these axes, we gain admiration from our audience. Neffinger and Kohut's work, based on earlier work by Cuddy, Fiske, and Glick, provides a useful taxonomy for these concepts. However, when working with my female leaders, I often see this as more of a continuum stretching from warmth at one end to strength at the other. I urge women to try to read their audience and engage with more warmth or more strength based on what the situation requires.

The most vivid example I can recall of this principle in action was in 1993, while Hillary Clinton was serving as First Lady and also leading the charge for health care reform. When seated at the senate hearings she would go toe to toe with the primarily male senate. She

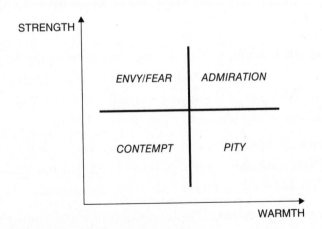

Figure 6.2 Strength/Warmth continuum
Source: *Compelling People,* Penguin Group, 2013.

was prepared, knew her data, and could answer point by point each charge they made. But on the breaks she did not drink coffee from a Styrofoam cup; instead, she had a small pot of tea. She would steep a tea bag, then enjoy her tea in a relatively dainty tea cup that her staff had provided. She seamlessly moved from strength to warmth in moments.

As a male ally and advocate for women leaders, I can only go so far. Allison, with her years of experience as a television producer and now university lecturer, can directly and candidly provide students even more. She begins with great research done by Katy Kay and Claire Shipman about how women are less likely to take risks in their careers. They describe how men are willing to apply for a job or promotion even if they have few of the qualifications, while women are unlikely to apply unless they have nearly 100 percent of the qualifications listed. Allison adds to this by saying, "Our biggest obstacle as women is that we have to just opt in and then figure it out." Allison sees the first step as convincing female leaders that they must apply for these roles and opportunities even if they do not feel they have 100 percent of the qualifications listed. (They likely have more than enough!). She then offers a slew of tips to enable women to be more effective communicators. She has agreed to let me offer several of them here:

1. **Grasp the landscape.** This is something Allison suggests women seem to do intuitively better than men; consider this your superpower. Take note of the setting, players, and issues, and use your knowledge of the terrain to navigate the meeting.

2. **Reduce the apologies.** Too often women apologize unnecessarily. Don't apologize as a way to start or end a conversation. Be accountable for your mistakes, but don't overcorrect.

3. **Accept compliments.** Allison uses a great Amy Schumer video clip to emphasize the self-diminishing impact of not being able to accept a compliment. (You can find it by searching Amy

Schumer's name and "compliments.") Accept and respond to a compliment so that you can own your own power.

4. **Use humor.** Often the warmest way to diffuse a tough situation is through humor. Allison suggests comments like, "John, that sounded really good when I said it ten minutes ago" to remind people of your efforts.

5. **Manage the interruptions.** Research shows that men are more likely to interrupt women than the other way around; prepare for that, preempt it when you can, and call it out gently and firmly when it still occurs. (Humor can help here, too.) See Kara's earlier sidebar on interruption for some additional strategies.

6. **Speak with certainty.** By eliminating qualifying phrases like "perhaps," "maybe," and "kind of," women can speak with greater certainty. It's better, Allison advises, to speak decisively than to waffle.

7. **Secure a mentor.** While many firms and sectors still have a poor record of advancing women to senior leadership, there are more role models today than ever before. Seek out a leader whose style you respect and whose success you admire. Ask for time to be formally or informally mentored as you move up in your career.

8. **Reflect and iterate.** We only get better at skills like this if we commit to growing with each new experience. Just like mastery, perfection never comes, but you can get incrementally better if you build in time to reflect and self-critique after key leadership communication experiences. Consider both what went well and what you can do differently next time. Commit to what you want to start, stop, and continue doing so that over time your presence continues to expand.

Beyond the strategies above, both Allison and Stephanie remind students of the basics of presence. Above all, do nothing to distract from your message: reduce fidgeting and any physical tics like adjusting your clothing or hair. And take simple actions to emphasize your message: crisp, clear gestures; direct eye contact; well-structured answers; and a concise summary of next steps. All of these actions apply equally to men and women, but the scrutiny, somehow, remains higher for women in the workplace.

I'll offer a final story to illustrate what I mean here. For one academic year I reduced my teaching load at Stanford to accept an appointment with Columbia University. My role was to lead the launch of their West Coast presence in San Francisco's financial district. One night, I needed to be at Columbia's San Francisco office to introduce a highly subscribed alumni event. As it turns out, my husband and I did not have child care that night, so I brought my then-six-month-old son Joshua with me. Of course, I put him into his baby blue Columbia onesie for the evening. He's a charmer and people were delighted to have him with me. When it came time to do my brief introduction, however, he was fussy. Try as they may, my colleagues could not calm him. So I simply took him in my arms, calmed him in the way only a parent knows to do, and walked forward to do my introduction. I spoke for maybe five minutes max, and then handed the evening off to the alumni leaders. I never commented upon the infant in my arms, and did not apologize for his presence. I simply did what I had committed to do for the evening. Later one of the local leaders told me she could never have done that.

"Do what?" I asked. "Bring your child with you to a work event?" She said, "No—do it without profusely apologizing for him."

That discrepancy had never crossed my mind. After that exchange, I did go through the evening newly aware that I had been given much more generous understanding than a female colleague would have received. The double standard, regrettably, remains. As long as it does, I'm glad I have colleagues with expertise like Stephanie and Allison, who can provide wisdom about the unique challenges women face when leading.

Leading as a Rookie

As my students graduate and begin their post-business-school careers, they share the experience of becoming "rookies" once again. Conventional wisdom tells us to quickly get past the rookie stage of our careers and grow into something more "elevated and respected."

I'm going to buck conventional wisdom here and suggest that being a rookie offers some incredible advantages that new employees should use while they can. Your early weeks in a new role represent a honeymoon period; the company wooed you, and now they have you. Remember that you aren't expected to know everything right away; this gives you the opportunity to develop the habit of asking questions and seeking out mentors who will likely be eager to assist you. I recall a friend's parent who moved beyond the old dinnertime question, "What did you do today?" and instead asked, "What questions did you ask today?" With that as your mindset, you'll build more relationships and learn more about your new environment early on.

Think of this time as an opportunity to start fresh with new habits. You can create new habits (like zeroing your inbox every day or practicing yoga over lunch) as you start a new job. Unlike New Year's resolutions, which can often go awry, new practices that you build into your work week can become habits. *Switch* by Chip and Dan Heath is a phenomenal guide to making personal and professional changes when change is hard.

To leverage these advantages, consider a few strategies:

Develop Allies Before You Need Them

My colleague Steve Mellas calls this "putting cookies into the jar before you take any out." Build a network by helping others; learn about their needs and priorities, and support their objectives while still getting your work done.

Embrace Your Confusion If You Don't Know What to Do

Many new managers try to deny or hide that they don't have an immediate answer to a vexing problem. While it's important not to appear weak, a rookie can pose questions that others who have been at the workplace longer may be either afraid to ask, or have simply never considered.

Learn from Your Cringe Moments

We've all had those moments when we realize we've made a huge mistake, and it's clear to many that we've goofed. Mellas and I termed these "cringe moments," while Jentz and Murphy call them "oh no moments" (ostensibly because no editor would allow them the scatological language they really wanted to use!). We make mistakes worse if we don't stop to learn from them, and cringe moments are the best teachers. Don't miss these lessons.

Limit References to the Past

We've all experienced the person who begins too many sentences with, "When I was at my old firm, we did it this way." While your new firm hired you in part for your past experience, decide when and how often you need to use the name of the school or firm you came from. Doing so can provide context when you have a relevant comparison to offer or important experience to share, but otherwise it can read as a defensive compensation for your lack of security in your new role.

Avoid Considering Differences as "Wrong"

Just because your past experience reflected a different way to process expense reports or celebrate retirements doesn't mean that your new firm's traditions are incorrect; they're simply different. Resist the urge to cast the "new" as "bad." Sometimes you may be right, but keeping these observations as silent reflections will help you to continue to build relationships, stay open to new ideas, and become a more fully integrated member of your new team.

Leading as a Military Veteran

One of my favorite audiences to serve each year is former (or transitioning) leaders from the armed forces. As the son of a WWII bronze star recipient and sibling of a career Army officer (now retired and working as an amazing mom), it's a privilege to give back to this distinct group of leaders in a meaningful way after all they've done for us. When first approached to tailor my content for this audience in the summer of 2014, I was not sure why we were offering a special summer institute for veterans who had served in the military after 9/11. Yet I came to learn that these leaders often struggle to translate their unique skills into civilian terms and face negative stereotypes and biases that can thwart their career success. Once I began to work with these remarkable men and women, they quickly became one of my favorite communities to teach. (I know. I know. Just like parents, we're not supposed to have our favorites, but these men and women are my favorites!) In fact, my colleague Bethany Coates became so taken with this group that she left her position at Stanford to found BreakLine, a social venture dedicated to offering veterans education and support to pivot into a post-military career.

Let me be clear: the work we do together is not about remediation. These men and women already possess remarkable skills from which any firm would benefit. Our work provides them the tools in their toolbox to translate these skills meaningfully. Regrettably, the Veteran's Administration called their post-military skills program "Vocational Rehabilitation"; one vet, Audrey Adams, pointed out that this term is elsewhere defined as "a process which enables persons with functional, psychological, developmental, cognitive, and emotional disabilities or impairments or health disabilities to overcome barriers to accessing, maintaining, or returning to employment or other useful occupation." That view sustains a narrative of "less than" that's simply not been my experience with this exceptional community. But it is clear that many veterans, who've been steeped in a tradition of humility and team esprit de corps, do need some guidance in navigating the nuances of a job search and the civilian world.

While I believe the entire book in your hands can be of help to veterans, I have also developed specific communication strategies for this population to ensure their success in career transition.

Connect the Dots

It won't be easy for a prospective employer without military experience (or experience with veterans) to translate veterans' skills to their opportunities. The veterans must quickly become agile at doing this themselves. It's often said that veterans' "career opportunities need not be limited to just defense contractors." In fact, I'd go one step further and say we need your skills even more in fields beyond defense contracting.

Promote Yourself

The vets with whom I've worked are not only quite talented, but they have also been steeped in humility. I was unaware of how central this quality is to the military experience before I began working with this group. In the military it's "service before self." As one leader, Charles Cathlin, told me: "Every sailor, soldier, or airman must work together and be prepared to step in and lead when called to do so, for purposes of a common mission. No matter your background or beliefs, you integrate into the military culture while leaving some of your individualism behind. This is almost the antithesis of individualism and building a 'personal brand' for yourself."

So although it is important to promote yourself when reentering the workforce, I urge this group of leaders not to swing too far from humble to arrogant, as that won't serve them either. Instead, I suggest that they take clear stock of their distinct talents and abilities, not shy away from detailing them on their résumés and LinkedIn profiles, and find stories that illustrate their talents for conversations with prospective employers. I was surprised to learn that one of the best places to find this data was leaders' past performance reviews. In the private sector, I don't know that I ever gave this advice; it might make sense to review performance reviews for self-promotion material there too, but in the military it absolutely does. These documents capture, often at a granular level, the specific impact a leader had on the mission or unit. If you do choose an excerpt from a performance review, Cathlin reminds us that the excerpt should be "jargon-free and use terms applicable to the position [you] seek."

Reduce the Acronyms and Jargon

Lots of fields love their acronyms, but none as much as the military; as an outsider, it's truly like communicating with someone in another language when military leaders drop terminology and acronyms without filtering. Not only does this confuse a civilian audience, but it can signal an inability to connect well with others if an applicant cannot shut off the use of these TLAs. (See what I mean? TLA stands for "three-letter acronym," but wasn't it annoying to have to read this parenthetical explanation to find that out?)

When I share this tip with students, I tell the story of my sister, who recognized the lunacy of too many acronyms when navigating the intersection of academia and the military. She had been assigned to teach ROTC at the University of Oklahoma in Norman and was looking forward to the role until she saw her name on the proof for her new business cards: Captain Kathy Schramm, PMS. Apparently men had mostly held the role of Professor of Military Science and did not object to the acronym. My sister found creative ways around it, or used it as a chance for laughter in interactions with students and colleagues on campus.

Counter Stereotypes with Positive Examples

Without giving too much energy to the potential negative stereotypes, I do encourage veterans to acknowledge in their prep that at least some employers may subscribe to these stereotypes, and they should seek to share experiences and stories to the contrary. For example, many of the leaders I've coached will emphasize the military traits of being "mission focused" and "humble," noting that they have these qualities specifically because of their military training.

Another veteran, Nathaniel Gilman, shared: "During my time as a service member, my mission every day was very clear. Protect the American people. Protect my crew. Protect my watch. Every day was filled with some kind of high-risk operations where someone could literally die. A difference that many of my friends deal with is they do not know what they are working for. The people I have seen be the most successful are able to find jobs where they believe in the mission."

While I do believe the bias against hiring veterans is waning, these leaders will still encounter some firms or individuals who don't embrace their service because of these biases. In these cases, I simply advise: If with your best efforts you cannot overcome that bias, then look for another firm; they frankly don't deserve somebody of your caliber. This leads us directly to my next tip.

Seek the Proper Fit

I believe career search is much like dating: both parties have to be happy with the match. Interviewing today is not just about getting a job, but determining whether you fit in that organization too.

In large organizations there may be a veterans' ERG (Employee Resource Group, showing that the private sector also uses too many TLAs), which can be a great help in determining fit. Absent that, I urge leaders to inquire candidly about work hours, team versus individual focus, advancement strategies, and day-to-day culture. While using tools like LinkedIn or Glassdoor are great, nothing beats having conversations directly with the people who will be your peers and the person who will supervise your work. Do not hesitate to take your time here, as a proper fit is crucial. Requesting one more meeting with the team is not unrealistic.

In my own career, I was considered for several internal transfers at Kaplan Educational Centers when my role in San Francisco was eliminated. For me, my decision came down to two options: Denver or Boston. Both roles paid about the same. Denver had greater supervision of full-time staff, while Boston had a clear focus on academics and supervising part-time teachers. What ultimately made the decision easy was that the regional director of the Denver opportunity interviewed me in Chicago, never letting me meet the team I'd be leading. Conversely, Rob Waldron, the regional director for Boston, brought me in and even let me participate in several staff events before making my decision. I had to assess my fit with the role, and I could not do that from afar or on a website. I needed to have specific conversations with individuals to do that. Boston it was.

Negotiate for Your Value

While I don't teach negotiation directly, I urge all of my leaders to pay attention closely when my faculty colleagues teach this subject. These lessons are crucial. As Audrey Adams, a U.S. Navy Officer, notes, we are often "encouraged to do the employment equivalent of marrying the first girl that kisses you." Military leaders who have operated on a clear and unambiguous pay scale system are often ill equipped to negotiate after the first civilian offer is made. If the offer comes on top of somebody already feeling less-than, it's hard to break with past experience and ask for more.

Further, some employers may lowball a veteran, knowing they have retirement benefits. That's just as unethical as increasing a man's pay because he has "a wife and kids to support," even though this still occurs from time to time. Veterans who've taken strong inventory of their assets and talents must be willing and confident to go a round or two of negotiation for a firm they want to join. So very much of our future earnings are pegged to our current earnings. This first civilian starting salary may be the most important time to negotiate.

Expect the Adjustment

With all that, I remind our veterans of the obvious: you still need to expect some adjustment, and in some cases, radical adjustment. Here is where the advice I offered in our conversation about rookie leadership comes back into play: above all, hold on to the mantra "different is just different; not good or bad." If veterans have a judgment on all things civilian in their workplace, it will be a pretty rocky road for them and their peers. Further, if a vet continues to say "back in the army" or worse yet "at my last duty station," it will get old for those with whom they work. I invite vets to journal about the differences they see to capture and learn from these differences. It helps to have a group with whom to share these insights (besides your partner!). These can be formal support groups of transitioning service members or simply informal groups you assemble yourself from friends with whom you used to serve. It's important that these not simply be gripe sessions, but that they move toward action. Asking the question, "So what?" can help. In other words: "So, got it, thanks, but what can you do about it?"

Nathaniel Gilman, referenced above, shared that the difference in the pace of work was ultimately too much for him to bear. "This is one of the main reasons I have decided to start my own business as well as consult on the side. I make my own hours and I do not feel like I am judged negatively by others when I start early and keep working late when required. In that same breath, if there is nothing going on, I am strongly against a 'butt in seat' policy. If there is no work to do, you should be out working on something else either personal or for the company." Unsurprisingly, he took his direct service experience with poor paperwork management and co-founded Mariner Credential Service, which streamlines the complex credentialing process for mariners by tracking licenses and professional development on the cloud.

If after reflection you find that the adjustment is still too uncomfortable, try thinking outside the box about what else you might do to forge your own career path.

Part 3 Scaling Your Leadership: The Communication Coaching Process

I've been blessed to work with hundreds of coaches and workshop leaders during my time at Stanford. Some come for one or two days each year, others work seasonally, and a few are nearly full time. It's abundantly clear to me that you cannot improve your communication skills simply by reading a book, any more than you can learn to swim by sitting in the bleachers (or worse yet, in the library!). As we've mentioned several times, communication mastery is about getting better and better at speaking and writing each time you communicate. Without a coach, you may simply be reinforcing bad habits, creating even more to unlearn when you really need to step up as leader with a larger span of influence. Just as clinical psychologist Meg Jay tells Millennials in her 2013 TED talk that "the time to start working on your marriage is before you are in one," I believe the best time to start working on your leadership communication skills is before you are leading a large enterprise. I cringe when I get a call from a former student saying something like, "I should have paid more attention in your class, and now I really need your help."

But I rejoice when a former student reaches out saying, "I'd love to have you or one of your coaches come work with my new team."

The prior two sections of our book are full of frameworks, lessons, and tips to expand your mastery of communication. This section is designed to allow you to transform the information into actionable steps to directly improve your speaking and writing and the skills of your direct reports, colleagues, and mentees. First, we'll focus on how to be coached, then how to coach others, and finally how to create a culture that embraces communication coaching.

7 When Being Coached

We're often asked what factors into a very successful coaching engagement. Each coaching engagement differs, but one thing that all successful coaching relationships share is an active and engaged participant. In this chapter, we offer some ways to maximize your effective engagement with your communication coach so you can meet your goals effectively: establishing your goals, selecting your coach, and adopting a coaching mindset.

Establishing Your Goals

Kara and I debated the order of these first two elements—establishing your goals and selecting a coach—but ultimately settled on beginning with goal setting. You've got to know what you want to accomplish before you engage a coach, even though you will likely have to refine those goals once you begin work with a coach.

Reading this book may be a great first step; you may now see developmental areas in sharper relief than before. If you felt a chill or recalled a bad experience while reading the preceding two sections of this book, you may already have identified a good starting point for the work you want to do. As we suggested in our discussion of leadership for veterans, looking at recent performance reviews may also help point to areas where you want to improve.

You can certainly also survey colleagues and supervisors, but be careful with that tactic. Many times we'll hear, "Oh, you're fine, stop worrying. I wish I wrote as well as you did." This may feel good, but as a springboard for improvement, it doesn't offer us anything valuable. Or you may get the opposite reaction, leaving you bowled over by a long list of skills to improve that resembles the table of contents of this entire book. Seek out a few trusted mentors and peers and have an informal conversation to seek insights into where your communication performance could be stronger. While new beginnings are a good time to focus on this (new years, new jobs, new budget cycles), don't put off starting work on your communication development.

Since the fall of 2007, all incoming MBA students at Stanford have been assigned a professional communication coach to work with them on writing, speaking, and participating in class for the entire first quarter of their studies. This substantial commitment by the GSB highlights the importance we place on clear speaking and writing for leaders. To my knowledge, no other business school has followed our lead yet, and it's been over 12 years now. In the first meeting with their coach we ask students to come in with some goals. Though the coach almost always has suggestions for students to consider as well, the students' goal setting is essential: not only to chart the course for the coaching engagement, but to provide the crucial motivation and ownership necessary for them to engage in the work.

But as you consider your coaching goals, remember to stay flexible. One veteran Stanford coach, David Schweidel, says that coaching a leader is like "being willing to cook an idea as you serve it and put it out there and let it be tested. It's all about how to disagree constructively. That involves not being attached to your version of what's best: strong ideas loosely held. I try to get people to advocate their position as forcefully as possible, and then be totally open and willing to consider all refutations and adjustments and counterarguments. And for some students, that's a huge leap for a lot of different reasons."

In that spirit, I urge leaders to set a few specific goals they wish to achieve through coaching—perhaps three. Then they might begin to look for a coach with expertise aligned with those goals, but to not be too rigidly attached, as David suggests. Your goals may change once you begin working with a coach who has a different perspective on your challenges and knows more about how to approach them than you do.

Selecting Your Coach

Knowing that unlike our GSB students, most of you won't be so lucky to have a coach assigned to you, we recognize that you will need to both identify and then select a coach. In some metropolitan areas there may be a network like the International Association of Business Communicators, which may allow you to find suitable possibilities. You may also want to contact local colleges or universities to see whether they have adjunct faculty who do this work as well. You might reference the directories of two well-regarded coach training and accreditation organizations, ICF (International Coach Federation) found at coachfederation.org, and IAC (International Association of Coaching) found at certifiedcoach.org. However, it's important to be true to your own goals in this area. Many of the coaches on these lists practice traditional executive coaching or life coaching, which can be broader and less helpful than you want for the skills we describe in this book.

For me, the best way to find suitable coaches has been by word of mouth. Ask colleagues if they have suggestions or see whether your HR office maintains a list of approved vendors for coaching. If it doesn't feel too risky to you, put a note out on LinkedIn or your company's Slack channel. We do this to seek for childcare suggestions; why not use the networks near us for self-care too?

Once you've found a coach (or a few), see whether you can meet in person once without cost. Some of the more established coaches may not be able to do this for free, but it's worth asking. Bring to the meeting not just your list of goals, but perhaps some examples of your work. If you have a few documents you've written or a short video of you presenting, share this with the coach and ask how they'd approach coaching you. As you assess the reply, pay attention to both content and chemistry. Do the suggestions offered make sense to you? If you could improve in that specific area, would it serve you to have help? But just as important, consider how the advice makes you feel. Do you feel honored and guided? Or do you feel too criticized? It's a very vulnerable step to offer ourselves to another in this way; you want to do your best to ascertain whether this relationship will inspire you to do more.

I will readily admit I've not spent much time inside of a gym; photos of me may support this admission. But I vividly recall a time in my thirties when I was a gym regular. I joined a gym in Boston's South End and began to explore options for a personal trainer. While I was tempted to simply choose one whom I found attractive (bad strategy), I ultimately chose one who had a great balance of challenge and encouragement. I needed both qualities to accomplish the goals I set for myself. With his coaching I was able to complete several long-distance bike rides and stay in reasonable shape for years, even after moving away from Boston and that gym.

Finally, ask for references. Has the coach worked with clients who had similar goals and were satisfied with the coaching they received? Can you speak directly with them? Choosing a communication coach can be a financial investment, but moreover it's a time investment. You want to be sure of your choice of coach before you get too far down the road getting feedback on your communication style.

Adopting a Coaching Mindset

When you're being coached on writing, speaking, or a combination
of both, it's important to keep an open mind, to take risks, and to
try the techniques your coach recommends before disregarding them.
Strategies that are new can feel effortful, silly, or strange, and ultimately you may not choose to use the techniques your coach suggests.
But without trying, you'll never know what might provide you the
key to improvement. To use one of many available sports analogies:
I've been to many football games, but I've never seen a single dis-
carded tire on the field. Yet I know that nearly every coach has their
players practice by running through tires. There will be parts of your
coaching that exist like "tires on a football field." A talented coach
may have you engage in activities or exercises focused on helping you
develop, but they may not be directly tied to the final product you are
working on. Trust your coach.

As we mentioned before, coaching is a gift, not remediation. The
higher you climb in your career and organization, the more likely it
is that you will want and encounter more varied coaches. Borrow-
ing from the sports arena again: It's more likely that an elite athlete
will have diverse coaches than a casual weekend athlete will. Serena
Williams likely has not only a hitting coach but also a condition-
ing coach, a nutritionist, and a strategy coach. At Google, executive
coaching is offered as a gift to senior, high-potential leaders with
specific skill investments that interest them. Coaching rewards potential; it's not an intervention for wrongdoing or lack of skill. You might
also adopt this view of coaching. The best coaching places you on the
shoulders of the leadership you've offered before, giving you new tools
to do so. It is a gift.

For the best results, you'll want to develop a relationship with
a coach over a period of time. That period may be a few weeks or a
few months or even a few years, depending on your bandwidth and
on the scope of the skill you're building. This allows your coach to

know your strengths and opportunity areas more intimately, and allows you to build increasing trust in your coach. One of the coaches I've worked with for over a decade now, Debbie Denenberg, knows my writing so well that each time we collaborate, she can help me improve with fewer cues and suggestions.

At the risk of reiterating this point too much, reiteration will be central to your successful coaching engagement. It's the virtuous cycle of feedback and practice, feedback and practice that will allow a leader to get the greatest benefit from coaching. Simply put: the more you put in, the more you'll get out. If you show up to a race having just used your speed techniques once, you'll be operating at a level of conscious competence at best. But if you practice repeatedly, you'll be able to refine your technique, hone your muscle memory so that the effort is less difficult, and feel confident that you've done all you can to ensure your best performance.

8 When Coaching Others

To offer world-class communication tools to our students at the GSB, we rely not only on our excellent faculty but also on a group of exceptional coaches. But you don't have to have the word "coach" in your title to guide those around you toward their best leadership communication styles. In this chapter, we explore some of the behaviors, attitudes, and tools that make a coach truly effective.

What Makes a Great Coach?

While some may argue that coaches should always be external to an organization, we believe the best leaders need to also step in to coaching their employees on a consistent basis. This requires a leader to clearly distinguish between ongoing coaching conversations and performance review conversations. This bifurcation is challenging, but the best leaders are able to do it masterfully. To coach others effectively, you need to exhibit:

- **Patience.** Remember that what is obvious to you may not be obvious to the people you are coaching. Not only are they gaining familiarity with a new skill, but they will likely be reconciling their previous way of communicating with a new approach. Ego, team dynamics, stress, and myriad other factors can contribute to the ease and pace at which someone adapts to coaching. Be patient and meet the people you're coaching where they are.

- **A focus on process over product.** A good writing coach will invest in asking leading questions to help the writer recognize opportunities for change, rather than editing the document. Lauren LaFauci, a coach from our very first year, used to regularly remind us to coach writing "without lifting a pen." Instead, she reminded us to ask probing questions of the writers to allow them to see choices in their writing. A good presentation coach won't give line readings of correct pronunciation or delivery, but instead will draw the best qualities out of the presenter. A focus on process over product means that the leader will be able to repeat the skill in the future, amplifying your impact as a coach across many opportunities rather than just one in a single coaching session. Focus on process to maximize your coaching value.

- **Flexibility and creativity.** In a coaching interview, Kara once received an unexpected question: "What's your coaching philosophy?" We both have a number of coaching philosophies—many of which you now know!—but in that moment, she chose "Make a plan and be flexible." And indeed, that philosophy is central to successfully coaching another person. While you should always have a confident vision of where the coaching engagement and each coaching session are headed, a great coach will demonstrate full willingness to scrap the plan and address the issues that are top of mind for the leader. If one technique doesn't appear to be a good fit, try another. If one parallel isn't landing, see whether you can create another way to explain the idea. You need not bend over backward to accommodate every issue you encounter, but adopting a mindset of flexibility and creativity will allow you many options for engaging with the person you're coaching.

- **Focus on the person you're coaching, not on yourself.** Our colleague Burt Alper talks about the importance of allowing those you're coaching a chance in the spotlight, even if you're better at the skill you're modeling. If you don't let leaders develop through practice, they won't. You will be better at the skills you are offering to the leaders you work with, and it will be valuable to model their use for clarity. But then, step back. Let them practice. Let the work be theirs. Let the words be theirs. Empower them to use the new skill partly your way and partly their way so that it feels authentic, repeatable, and effective.

- **Empathy.** Ultimately, we coach communication skills because they're what connect us to each other. You don't need us to tell you that life is complicated, or that each person you meet has challenges, history, and perspectives you may never know. Your coaching relationship is just one small chapter in the leader's experience. It may bring up issues of identity, worthiness, purpose, or fear. Be as empathetic as you can in recognition that the coaching process is personal, and that what is personal can be sensitive. Slow down, listen, and let the leaders you're coaching engage in the material in the way they need.

Defining the Coaching Role

When you first sit down with a new coaching client, mentee, or colleague, it's invaluable to set the expectations for your coaching work together. We've established that a good coach is patient, flexible, creative, focused on process and the leader, and empathetic. But it's also helpful to define what a good coach is *not*. Ideally, as a coach you should not be an editor, a ghost writer, a content creator, a philosopher, or a psychologist (although you may have moments of dipping lightly into each of these areas occasionally, depending on your experience). You are there to guide leaders with new tools, new approaches, and new skills that they can use to communicate

effectively. Together you may decide that you have a particular finish line—for example, an upcoming keynote at which the leader is
presenting, or a manuscript someone is contracted to complete—
but your focus should not be on completing the goal for the leaders as much as outfitting them to do the work themselves, with
your guidance.

The sooner you can agree on logistics, the better. How often
will you meet, for how long, and where? Many people prefer to hold
coaching sessions in a private place where it's more comfortable to
share proprietary information, try vulnerable exercises, or practice
presenting. A whiteboard can be useful for working through some
of the frameworks we've shared throughout this book, or simply for
brainstorming. Meeting cadence varies depending on availability and
goals, but we find that an every-other-week meeting schedule offers
a good middle ground between giving leaders time to practice and
maintaining momentum between sessions. An hour might be a good
sweet spot for the length of these meetings. While some of our colleagues can accomplish a lot in just half an hour, we find that an hour
allows ample practice and clarification time. More than an hour, and
you may find that attention starts to wane. Regardless of what you
decide for location, cadence, and session length, agree up front so that
the terms are clear.

Tools of the Trade

Truthfully, our coaching toolboxes are overflowing with approaches
we've learned from our colleagues, developed through our own experiences, and gleaned from teachers and researchers. But in this section,
we've pared our suggestions down to the tools we come back to again
and again: video feedback, coaching exercises, the coach's parking
lot, and community. With these four tools in your pocket, you will
be well on your way to offering others effective routes to clear communication.

Video Feedback

There are coaches who will immediately play back video and review it with leaders. In fact Linda Cappello, our coach-in-residence at the GSB, holds weekly office hours in a video studio for just this purpose. I have always preferred to provide students with video, then encourage them to go through a three- or four-step review process on their own. Irv Schenkler developed a useful framework for this process—adapted from Lynn Russell's "Refine Your Delivery"—that I often offer.

Step One: First, watch once to get all of your "dislikes" out of the way. Many of us find it uncomfortable to watch ourselves on video, and as a result we become distracted by things we wish were otherwise. Take one pass of your video to get over the fact that your sweater doesn't fit quite right, that you coughed right in the middle of your sentence, or that you wore the wrong shoes. Now that that's out of the way, let's move on to step two.

Step Two: Watch once with the video off to focus solely on your verbal and vocal communication. How well are your word choices, the order of your content, and your distribution of evidence serving your message? How clear is your enunciation? What is your volume like? What about your vocal variety? Take notes about what you notice.

Step Three: Now watch the video once with the audio off to evaluate your non-verbal communication. How are your gestures? Are you planted, swaying from side to side, or walking in a distracting way? What do your slides or props add or subtract from the presentation? How is your eye contact with the audience?

Step Four: Now, though this is often the hardest part for many of us, force yourself to identify everything and anything that you *like* about your presentation and your delivery of it. Consider the verbal, the vocal, and the visual. Perhaps your audience laughed, applauded, or asked questions in a place that signaled good resonance. How was your body language, your vocal quality, your ability to end on time or interact with your slides? Note the times your stance looked solid or your inflection communicated gravitas. Jot down all of these positive elements. You may be able to double down on what you're doing well and use those techniques more in the future.

A great tool for video feedback is GoReact. I've begun to expand its use in my classes and with my private clients. GoReact takes any format of video input and places it into an easy-to-use platform for feedback. Once the video is loaded I can begin to review the talk. When I feel compelled to offer a comment, like, "Great opening story, work to be more concise," I can start typing and the video will pause while I type. Once I hit enter, the video continues to play. If you wish to implement this tool more elaborately, you might encourage peers to give one another feedback using the tool, even simulcasting so audience members can type feedback in the moment as the talk occurs.

When coaching, I will often record the in-the-moment feedback that I offer leaders so that they won't have to take heavy notes while we're in conversation. Because of the work I do in my career, almost everything I hear transforms into a plus/delta list in my head. I've even been known to pass a cocktail napkin of plus/deltas to people who offer a toast at a wedding so they know what they did well and how they might improve on future toasts! As we mentioned in our discussion of synthesis and its superiority over summary, less can be more when it comes to feedback—and folding it into the video that a leader will review can be a valuable part of the streamlining process.

Coaching Exercises

We could write a whole other book about communication coaching exercises (and maybe one day we will!), but here are a few that will give you a sense of how actionable, iterative exercises can build new skills over time.

- **Reducing content to its essence.** Our students are often amazed how few words it takes to communicate the essence of a message. Here's an exercise that Kara uses with clients to challenge them to distill a message to its essentials: Find a brief movie or book synopsis (any issue of the *New Yorker* will have dozens) and ask the person you're coaching to read it. Now ask them to edit the synopsis down to 100 words. Next, ask them to edit it down to 50 words. Then, 25. Can it go down to 10? They will discover that many adverbs, adjectives, verb phrases, and fillers are not necessary for conveying the essential summary. This exercise will heighten their sensitivity to using extra words in their own work. As a next step, invite them to repeat the exercise on an email, memo, or post that they have written.

- **Stop and start.** As coaches, it's our job to deliver feedback as close to the moment of impact as possible. As leaders begin to rehearse a presentation or try a skill, stop them when you see an area for improvement. Start again and stop again as necessary. This approach will not only offer the leaders more opportunities to practice; it will provide them extra sensitivity to the moments where they can improve.

- **Eye contact raising hand activity.** For those among us who have trouble maintaining eye contact or making eye contact with multiple people in a space, try this exercise. Ask everyone in the room to raise their hands while the presenter speaks. Only when the presenter has made firm, sustained eye contact of four to seven seconds with each audience member may that audience member lower his or her hand. This is an awkward exercise, but it underscores the worthwhile effort of connecting with an audience.

The Coach's Parking Lot

Chances are, if you're working with a leader on an extended coaching engagement, you'll cover a great deal of material and explore a wide range of nuance. While it is certainly not your job as the coach to be the scribe and keeper of these insights, many leaders find it helpful to have a shared, compiled, written record of their best practices, takeaways, and parking lot of topics to cover. (If you've never heard the term "parking lot" used in this way before, we're referring to the place where we "park" unanswered questions, unbroached topics, or unmet goals until the appropriate time to address them. Many times these are collected on sticky notes on a flip chart and look like a "parking lot" from above.) In the weeks between sessions, they can use this document as a reference for ways to practice new skills; after the engagement has concluded, it can serve as a living document for leaders to refresh their toolkits or share with others who could benefit from the insights.

In her practice, Kara takes notes during individual sessions with clients, then sends them an electronic document (email, Quip, Google Doc, or otherwise) with a record of the day's salient conversation points, new skills, key takeaways, and best practices; ways to continue practice; and items left to cover in the parking lot. As a coach, this may help you to visualize a clear road map of where you've been with your client and where you are headed. It can also keep specific conversations fresh as you move from coaching one leader to another. Although not every coach will wish to take the time to offer this amenity, many leaders report that they continue to use this document for years after the coaching engagement has concluded—and it serves as a memory and planning resource for the coach as well.

If this idea appeals to you, consider creating a template that you can use to offer notes to those whom you coach.

Community

Whether you're a professional coach, a community leader, a solo practitioner, or a student, your greatest coaching asset will always be other people. Even if you've been trained at the same program or by the same people, everyone has a different approach to guiding others toward new skills.

A couple of years ago, I had an idea to invite my GSB coaching community to a lunch at the new San Francisco location for Columbia University, where I was teaching at that time. What started as a list of a dozen grew and grew as I recalled the many connections I'd made during my time at Stanford. Once the room was assembled, I asked everyone to speak briefly on their expertise and experience, but also to share one need with the group and one thing they were willing to share. The coaches asked for referrals, second opinions on tricky client issues, resources and book ideas, exercises to try, and even feedback groups for professional development. In return, they offered their specialized skill sets, a second pair of eyes on a document, camaraderie through lunches or coffees, introductions to clients and professional groups, and more. I was blown away by the diversity and richness of resources that existed just within that room. If that was the result of a single hour over salads in a classroom, what could we do with an ongoing network of connections over the years to come?

You need not bring your community together in this semi-formal way, as I did. Simply thinking of your peers and colleagues as a source of learning, growth, and new ideas is an empowering place to start. Solicit their feedback and offer your own. Consider what you may have to trade someone from your own portfolio of expertise. Much coaching is done one-on-one, but the best coaching is not solitary. It exists in community, as we do.

9 Creating a Coaching Culture

By now you know that no great coaching relationship can exist in a vacuum. As with any endeavor we undertake, we excel when we operate within a culture that's conducive to our success. So what kind of culture promotes coaching success? We can promote radical candor in our organizations, model and mirror the behaviors we hope others will try, and ensure that the right coaching is coming from (and to!) the right people. In this chapter, we tell you more about each of these key components to fostering a culture where coaching relationships can grow.

Everyone Can Coach (But Not Everyone Should)

A few years ago, Kara had the lucky experience of working with a highly motivated client. Billie (not her real name), a senior director in a large tech organization, was not only excited to use the tools from her coaching sessions in her own leadership, but to offer them to her team. Nearly every time Kara and Billie would practice a new framework, stance, or approach, Billie would say, "I have *got* to get my team to try this!" (Music to a coach's ears—we *love* when being coached creates a coaching mindset.) So Billie asked Kara to write a "brief one-pager" of the exercises, techniques, and best practices from their work so that she could share it with her team.

Kara asked Billie, whose schedule was incredibly fast-paced, how she planned to find time to coach her team through the skills on this one-pager.

"Oh, they're super quick. They'll catch right on!" Billie said.

As you know since you've read this far in our book, even the smartest, most motivated leaders need dedicated practice, feedback, and iteration to approach mastery of a new skill. Kara and Billie had been working together long enough that Billie certainly could have coached her team through the materials—*if* she'd had the time and dedicated preparation to do so. But Billie had neither the flexibility in her schedule nor the luxury of sustained time to devote to her team's communication development *as a coach*. As their manager, Billie could offer her team awareness of their growth areas, insights into her own learning experiences, encouragement to pursue new skills, and resources to pursue them. Those are invaluable offerings. But they are the precursors, complements, and supports for coaching—they do not constitute the coaching experience itself.

Ultimately Kara and Billie concluded that the most valuable thing Billie could do to create a coaching culture in her team was to share her own experiences, model her new skills, and encourage and resource her team to pursue their own coaching. (She was fortunate to work at a company that values coaching as a learning and development asset.) Billie *could have* done some coaching on her own, but ultimately the best way for her to elevate her team's skills was to provide the scaffolding that made dedicated coaching possible.

Maintaining a clear distinction between skills coaching and offering a performance review can go a long way toward creating a culture open to coaching. As a leader, it's important to avoid saying, "May I offer you some coaching on this?" when you mean, "I need to give you feedback on your performance." Effective coaching must be divorced from performance evaluations, and should be offered in a non-threatening, risk-embracing setting. That's why, for the most part, leaders seek outside consultants or coaches to coach their teams.

Acknowledging and sharing results from your own personal coaching can also set a model for an effective coaching culture. When Jon Levin took over as the tenth dean at Stanford's GSB, I had the privilege of providing him coaching through a university program offered to senior leaders throughout the campus. At first I was very confidential about this relationship, wanting to protect Dean Levin's privacy. However, when I learned he was very open with others about the coaching he was receiving, I realized I need not feel sworn to secrecy. Of course, I never discussed the nature of our work together with others, but I was pleased to have such a high-profile client who was unabashed in embracing the value of coaching.

I vividly recall pushing him to use more storytelling in his talks at the GSB. He shared with me that he "didn't have any GSB stories," since he was neither a grad nor faculty member prior to being named as dean. I urged him to ask everybody he met in his first year to share a story with him, and in so doing, to become a collector of great stories. In his second year, during his second time offering the new student welcome, he began with two compelling and vivid stories from his travels. It was remarkable to see him so easily and quickly embrace the coaching I was offering. But his biggest contribution to the coaching culture of the GSB was his openness about his own experience and learning from working with a coach. The more open you can be about the coaching you receive, the more you will bake coaching into your own community's recipe for success.

Embracing Radical Candor

I had the pleasure of getting to know Kim Scott when she was working on the framework that would become the basis of her best-selling book *Radical Candor*. I wish every leader I know could embrace her style of giving feedback. It so brilliantly mirrors the spirit we've tried to capture in our discussion of coaching your team. Scott believes that there are two intersecting axes that provide the framework for effective feedback (Figure 9.1). We must both "care personally" and "challenge directly." Only when I am strong in both of these dimensions is radical candor possible. Once I understood these dimensions, I saw that her framework was ideal for coaching as well.

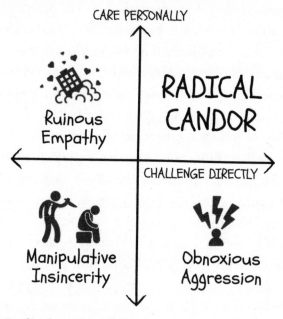

Figure 9.1 Radical candor chart
Source: The Radical Candor Framework is a trademark of Radical Candor, LLC.

Since learning Kim's framework, I've had numerous opportunities to use it. I will share a story about one time I did so successfully. Burt Alper has co-taught with me since 2013, when I revised the class and began to teach with others. Burt is a gifted speaker and talented coach for our students, but at that time, his work in presentation skills coaching was relatively new. He had spent much of his professional career in naming and branding and was moving into this arena for the first time when I hired him. I noticed that each time we began a class, Burt used self-deprecating humor in his introduction. I theorized that his choice was, in part, due to his relatively new status in the field. I was able to approach him in a manner that was both caring and direct. I shared that I found his self-deprecating humor hurt his credibility with the students unnecessarily. We strategized other options, and he adjusted immediately.

If I can interact with my team with both "caring directly" and "challenging personally" in mind, I can model the type of feedback they should offer to me and to each other. Admittedly, this is aspirational. At times, we may fail to challenge as directly as we would like. And there are colleagues about whom we may find it difficult to care personally; after all, we're only human. When my approach slips into the three non-optimal boxes of Kim's radical candor chart, her framework gives me the language to recognize where I am and where I wish to be. We have recommended many fine authors over the course of this book, but truly, Kim Scott's *Radical Candor* is one of those most important titles for leaders to read.

When I Should Have Used Radical Candor Earlier and More Effectively

Much of this book has been about my experiences at Stanford, but for one academic year I enjoyed faculty appointments at both Columbia and Stanford. I reduced my load at the GSB in order to accept a leadership role at Columbia, helping to launch their West Coast site in downtown San Francisco. It was a remarkably challenging year, but I learned so much about my own leadership style in both my successes and failures at the job.

(Continued)

I knew that neither Columbia nor Stanford (nor my husband, for that matter) wished to have me in joint roles for a second year. By the summer of 2019, I needed to choose to remain at Stanford or to exclusively work for Columbia. Week by week I would vacillate about which university I would serve the following year.

Finally, by March, several factors had combined to make it clear I would leave Columbia and not return for a second year. I chose to write a short three-page memo to my supervisor sharing many of the factors that led to my decision. I labored for days over that three-page document, wanting to strike the right tone, to be clear, and yet hoping to provide guidance that might make the role and reporting structure work more effectively after I left. I believe what I delivered was both "direct" and "caring."

However, I made one large error. Although I was successfully practicing radical candor with peers and direct reports, it was probably the *first* time I had practiced radical candor with those to whom I reported at Columbia. I had endured many disappointments without offering a single comment; nobody in the organization, particularly my two supervisors, had any idea of my feelings. Even though I had brought Kim Scott in to speak with a visiting class taught by our own dean, I had not embodied her principles until announcing my decision to leave. That was not fair to those who hired me.

Only later did I see that true radical candor is not simply how we manage those who report to us, but that it should also be how we interact with peers and supervisors. It should be something we use not just in moments of transition, but throughout our leadership. This will remain a missed opportunity, but incredibly profound professional lesson for me.

Mirroring and Modeling Best Practices

It's been said in many ways that the most sincere form of flattery is copying another's behavior. As we draw toward the end of this book, I hope you feel that you have a wide variety of best practices to model so that others may mirror your communication. As you consider the creation of your organization's coaching culture, think about your personal communication. What are you offering others, verbally or non-verbally, as a suggestion for how they might share their ideas and interact? The more you can embody the style that works best for you, the more passive coaching you will offer to your community.

EPILOGUE

IT'S IN YOUR HANDS NOW

So our book has been in your hands for the last few days, weeks, or months (ideally not years!) and now as we draw to a close, the next step is also in your hands. I often tell the leaders with whom I've worked that the time we've spent is a sunk cost. They won't get those hours back; the investment has been made.

Think of your journey with us, in reading this book, the same way. Your time has already been invested; you can only reap the dividends of your reading if you take action. My hope is that you will do just that: change how you communicate because of what you've gained here. More than that, I hope not only that you will commit to writing and speaking with greater mastery, but that you will inspire others on your team to do the same. As my friend James Buckhouse at Sequoia likes to say about storytelling: "The power is in retransmission. It's not the story you tell or the story they hear, but the story they retell that gives a leader power." We can apply that concept to leadership communication in all its facets: it's not the presentation you give, the report you write, or the message your audiences receive that matters; what matters is the message they both recall and retell. For years at the GSB we've told our student leaders that their ultimate communication goal should be to be heard (or read), understood, and remembered. We hope you'll do the same.

Here are some tips on how best to implement what we've offered here:

- **Start small and then expand.** Don't attempt to reshape all that you write and deliver. First set a few immediate attainable goals, then set further goals once you've begun to see some success.

- **Consider this book to be a buffer.** You don't have to try every-thing we suggest, and you don't have to like everything you try. Just as we train leaders at Stanford in a tailored and individual way, we hope you will adapt what we offer to your needs.

- **Visit and revisit this book often.** We have tried to provide both a clear table of contents and a rich index to make it easy to find frameworks or activities you want to deploy in your own communication; I hope you marked and highlighted your book as you read so you can quickly revisit the applications of our suggestions.

- **Recall Maslow's four elements of learning.** Gently move yourself from unconscious incompetence to unconscious competence, characteristic by characteristic.

- **Partner with somebody.** If you cannot invest in a coach, at least try to create an accountability partnership with somebody else to hold you to your commitment communication mastery. Con-sider establishing a reading circle for this book at work and move through the book systematically with others.

- **Visit my website.** I plan to use http://www.jdschramm.com /mastery to provide updated material and establish a community of readers committed to expanding their mastery of communica-tion. Particularly if you used the audio version of the book, you may find the website an effective way to further your understand-ing and use of the material.

The journey of writing this book has enabled us to clarify and codify the work of scores of colleagues and our work with thou-sands of students and clients. While many of us have written and spoken in different areas about our leadership communication efforts, never before have we put it all in one single place. That alone was a major feat and success. But our success will be realized when people not at the GSB, readers like you, begin to write and speak with greater conviction and effectiveness. That challenge lies in your hands, and we look forward to seeing what you do with what we've provided.

My original title for this book was *Approaching Mastery*. While our wise editors talked me into something more memorable and marketable, I want to leave you with a reminder of that concept. We can only *approach* mastery in communication; we cannot achieve it. With every email we write and every talk we deliver, we get incrementally better and better. That's what mastery is all about. Perfection is impossible, but growth is always attainable. I wish you the very best as you approach mastery in your own distinct way.

APPENDIX A

POWER VERBS

abandon	believe	consider	descend
absorb	bisect	constrain	describe
abstract	bombard	construct	design
accelerate	bond	construe	designate
access	broaden	contain	detail
accrue	calculate	continue	deteriorate
acknowledge	carry	contract	determine
activate	cease	contrast	devise
add to	cede	contribute	diagram
allow	challenge	converge	differentiate
alter	characterize	convert	disagree
analyze	circulate	create	discharge
apply	clarify	criticize	discover
appraise	classify	crystallize	discuss
argue	coalesce	curb	disintegrate
arrange	code	debate	disperse
ascend	collapse	decide	dissect
assemble	collect	deduce	disseminate
assert	color	define	distinguish
assess	combine	delineate	distribute
associate	compare	demonstrate	divide
assume	compose	depict	dominate
attribute	conclude	deposit	dramatize
behave	condense	derive	eliminate

elongate	identify	memorize	preview
emanate	illuminate	migrate	produce
emit	illustrate	minimize	propel
employ	imply	mix	propose
encompass	indicate	model	prove
enrich	infer	modify	provide
estimate	influence	name	question
evaluate	inform	narrate	quicken
evolve	insist	note	radiate
examine	inspect	observe	recall
exchange	interact	obtain	reclaim
exert	interlock	occur	recognize
experiment	interpret	operate	reconstruct
explain	introduce	order	record
express	invade	organize	regroup
expunge	inventory	orient	reiterate
extend	invert	originate	relate
extrapolate	investigate	overlap	remove
exude	invoke	overlie	rename
fill in	isolate	pattern	render
force	join	penetrate	reorganize
forecast	judge	permeate	repeat
form	lag	plan	repel
formulate	link	plunge	report
fracture	list	point out	represent
fuse	locate	postulate	require
generalize	maintain	practice	restate
group	manage	precede	restore
guide	maximize	predict	restrict
halt	mean	prepare	result
hypothesize	measure	present	reveal

review

rotate

rupture

saturate

scatter

schedule

separate

set forth

set up

show

simplify

sinter

sketch

slow

solve

specify

speculate

state

streamline

substitute

subtract

suggest

synthesize

summarize

superimpose

superpose

support

surmount

surround

symbolize

synthesize

systematize

take apart

terminate

test

think

transect

transfer

translate

transmit

traverse

trend

uncover

underlie

use

vary

verify

yield

APPENDIX B

MEMO ON THE QUALITY OF MEMOS

TO: Students in GSBGEN315 Strategic Communication

FROM: JD Schramm

DATE: February 20, 2020

RE: Providing Writing Guidance: A Memo on the Quality of Memos

We all look forward to reading your Prudential recommendations to management about issues of concern about Mark's choice. To help you prepare your revision (and future memos), we wanted to provide you some further guidance on business writing since the rest of our work will focus on oral communication in this course. By formatting this as an actual memo we hope to both model and articulate key information about writing effective and persuasive business documents. You could apply *nearly all* of this information to letters, emails, reports, and proposals. We will address items consistent with that which we used to evaluate your memos:

- Style and Format
- Technique and Grammar
- Content and Analysis

Additionally, we've provided information about the Microsoft Word readability statistics and how to use these to help you improve your writing.

Deploy a Powerful, yet Standard, Business Memo Format

Don't simply try to meet our personal preferences for business writing, but rather learn and understand what is meant by standard business style. Employers will often provide specific expectations within a firm. Learn and follow what's required of you. Below find the **memo standard** we provided for this course:

- Single-spaced
- Double-space between paragraphs; no indentation
- Left justify your document (not full justification)
- Serif type (11 or 12 point)
- Subheadings to guide the reader
- Intro/Sections/Conclusion
- Bullets for lists of **three or more** items
- Numeric lists when indicating a **process** or **priority** of bulleted items

As we've all reviewed student memos over the years, we found several style elements that we feel are important to add or emphasize.

1. Use a serif font (like the one you are reading) for any text that is dense; you can use sans serif fonts for headings or subheadings (as we've also done), but not for body text.

2. Apply left justification (again like this), not full justification, which can stretch and scrunch your words; business readers are used to a "ragged right edge" in a memo.

3. Avoid using bullets in front of full paragraphs as it loses the impact of setting off a list of items you wish to emphasize; use bullets for short phrases without punctuation.

4. Resist the urge to place headings (or subheadings) on each and every paragraph in a document; this reduces the flow of the document and begins to feel like you are shouting at the reader.

5. Leave more space above a heading than you have below it; a heading should not "float" equally between two sections, but should be closer to the paragraph it modifies.

Verify Proper Grammar

While deploying a strong format, it is vital to avoid spelling or grammar errors, as they could hurt your credibility. Be sure to proof (and at times have another person proof) your document carefully. Avoid misspelled words, but also avoid mixing up commonly confused words (e.g., fewer or less; between or among, etc.). Numerous web-based resources can help you master these items. JD's personal favorite site is http://owl.english.purdue.edu/.

In class we discussed that the most effective business writing is:

- Active—avoid the passive voice
- Brief—why say in ten words what can be said in three?
- Clear—reduce misunderstandings with clarity

Continue to hone your skills in these critical three areas of technique. Develop your skills in writing in a way that's Active, Brief, and Clear. Passive voice, in particular, seems to be challenging for many students. Measure this by considering the vividness of your verbs. If you include a great deal of "is/are" or "was/were" constructions in your writing, then you're probably writing in the passive voice too often.

Craft Persuasive Content

It still holds true that while style and technique matter, content remains king. Know your communication objective up front and write each section, each paragraph, and each line with this persuasive intent in mind. Recommendations or requests should be:

Easy to find. Offset the recommendations with bullets in a section where there are suggestions for change in the organization.

Easy to follow. Begin each recommendation with a specific and clear verb so that you provide the readers with a "recipe" for improving their performance.

Looking at past memos for this particular assignment, we found that many students are general or vague about their request of the reader. The entire memo is *about* the advice that you want to be first *read* and then *accepted*. Everything should lead to this. Re-read your memo as if you were the HR leader: would you be engaged?

Consider the Guidance from MSWord Readability Tools

Activate this tool by following the instructions in MSWord; it produces readability statistics.

We recommend you shoot for the following ranges in your business writing.

• Sentences per paragraph	Under 5
• Words per sentence	Under 17
• Characters per word	Under 5 (on average . . .)
• Passive Sentences	Low, fewer than 10 percent
• Flesch Reading Ease	High, over 40
• Flesch-Kincaid Grade Level	Low, in the single digits

These readability statistics serve **only as guidelines**; view these in context of each document's audience, intent, and message. They contain a margin of error, so only look at them for guidance, not as the final word on good writing. The readability index on this memo indicates a passive voice of 9 percent and an average sentence length of 17.2 words. (Trying to hold ourselves to the same standards we are expecting of you.)

Practice These Principles in All Your Affairs

Apply these concepts to all of your writing. **Your career carries much more weight than this course.** An executive or entrepreneur without the skill of strong persuasive writing will be at a severe disadvantage. Focusing on your written communication prowess will pay off in your future. As a short recap keep these principles in mind:

- Deploy a Powerful Business Memo Format
- Verify Proper Grammar
- Craft Persuasive Content
- Consider Readability Guidelines

Nearly all of this information applies to cover letters, emails, proposals, reports, and business letters, not just memos. Strong business writing will carry you far, while weak business writing may prove to be an obstacle for you. Please contact JD or your cohort coach if you have further questions.

APPENDIX C

MORE TIPS ON WINNING WRITING FROM GLENN KRAMON

These tips pick up from our conversation about writing earlier in the book. The whole document of Glenn's tips exists on my webpage. What follows are Glenn's words:

RULE ONE: The first thing to ask yourself is: Who is my audience? I know you know this, but I'm struck by how many times we forget it. Think first: What result do I want from this writing, and how can I persuade the reader to help me achieve it? What is my ask?

RULE TWO: Before you begin writing, it's so important to make sure you can answer this question: If you boiled it down to one phrase, sentence, or paragraph, what would it say? The shorter, the better. Put another way: Use the Miniskirt (or Speedo) Rule: *Make it long enough to cover the basics, but short enough to keep it interesting.*

◆ Use shorter, simpler words and sentences—*help* rather than *assist* or *facilitate, use* instead of *utilize, start* instead of *commence, improve* instead of *try to make better.* Pretend you're typing on your phone—it's so unpleasant to use those keyboards, you force yourself to say it in fewer words.

• "We are **in the process of** investigating." Why not "We are investigating"? And "I am **currently** working for Google" is better as "I work at Google."

- Use strong words. For example, why say "*she is incredibly smart*" when you can say "*she's brilliant.*" Why say something is "*extremely important*" when you can say it's "*crucial.*" And "*especially unusual*" is more powerful as "*rare*" or "*extraordinary.*" Indeed, remember that using too many adverbs is a sign of weak writing.

- Some examples where an adverb does NOT add value:
  - I **successfully** got a scholarship
  - I **completely** crushed it
  - **Tragically,** the train derailed, killing 100.
  - We're **absolutely** certain the election was rigged.
  - The gender gap **totally** disappeared.
  - Geeky men are **socially** awkward.

RULE THREE: Write it as you would say it to your colleague or friend. Avoid impersonal, abstract business jargon. Keep it simple.

- One trick: Say it to a friend and then write it as you said it. I'm surprised by how often a reporter can tell me a story better than she can write it. And once you've written it, read it aloud. Pretend you're delivering it to a friend or an audience. It will help you edit out unnecessary or unhelpful words. And it will help you sound less pretentious.

- Avoid business jargon: *encourage* instead of *incentivize, affected* instead of *impacted, carry out* instead of *implement.*

- Even worse is useless jargon, such as "I work in the ecommerce *space*" (what value does "space" add?). And "This was a crisis *situation*" (ditto for "situation"). And "we have an action plan" (what other kind of plan is there?).

RULE FOUR: Get to the point quickly, not at the end. People grow
impatient. Any of you appeared on TV? When the camera light
comes on, you have about three seconds to win or lose your audience. As our students in the military have learned when talking
to superiors: *"B.L.U.F.—Bottom Line Up Front."* Say the most
important things first.

APPENDIX D

THE LEADERSHIP COMMUNICATION BOOKSHELF

You are to be highly commended! Not only did you make it to the back of the book, but you are now reading the appendices. That's impressive. To acknowledge your effort, this appendix item is a synthesis of the bibliography to follow. In the bibliography we tried to be comprehensive, including all the books JD and Kara have referenced in this book and have used in our teaching and coaching.

But, as a shortcut, here are the ten books (besides the one in your hands) that we endorse the most for our students and clients. We've told you the title and author (the what) and why each title is relevant (the so what), so we will leave it to you to get the books into your own hands (the now what).

1. *Made to Stick: Why Some Ideas Survive and Others Die* by Chip and Dan Heath. Although it's been over 12 years since its publication, this book reset the bar for "sticky messages"—the goal of all leaders. Their SUCCESs model is key to *your* success in encouraging your audiences to recall and act on your message.

2. *The Credibility Code: How to Project Confidence and Competence When It Matters Most* by Cara Hale Alter. This slim book is the most practical guide to public speaking out there. Used in concert with her Google talk by the same name, these pages will be a great resource for you and your team to build confidence and presence.

3. ***Storytelling with Data: A Data Visualization Guide for Business Professionals*** by Cole Nussbaumer Knaflic. Knaflic has beautifully cut through the noise of bad charts and graphs and made a simple guide for all leaders who use data to persuade. She also has a website and podcast by the same name.

4. ***Presence: Bringing Your Boldest Self to Your Biggest Challenges*** by Amy Cuddy. Yes, I acknowledge there are those who question her research methods, but her findings work for me and my students. Don't just watch her 2012 TED talk; also read the book, which came out three years later. Her insights have helped millions of us speak with greater confidence.

5. ***Speaking Up Without Freaking Out*** by Matt Abrahams. Don't let the slim size of this book fool you. It's packed full of strategies and tips to help you exude confidence and reduce anxiety. It's one of the books my students always keep at the end of the quarter (or give to their team members when they enter leadership roles).

6. ***The Startup Pitch: A Proven Formula to Win Funding*** by Chris Lipp. As we noted in the section on pitching, Lipp's simple, straightforward approach not only makes sense, but makes pitching easier. Based on his own experience and research conducted at Tech Crunch and elsewhere, it's a must-have for any entrepreneur.

7. ***Illuminate: Ignite Change Through Speeches, Stories, Symbols, and Ceremonies*** by Nancy Duarte and Patti Sanchez. Okay, two of Duarte's books made this list, but I put this one first because it is the most comprehensive look at how to navigate the S-curve of change for you and your followers in your organization. The "centerfold" in this book is a crucial item to keep and reference moving forward.

8. ***Radical Candor: Be a Kick-Ass Boss Without Losing Your Humanity*** by Kim Scott. Scott's simple and actionable two-by-two matrix should be on the cover of every performance review

manual in the world. She calls you to consider how you can both care personally and challenge directly when giving feedback. A must-read for all leaders!

9. ***Resonate: Present Visual Stories That Transform Audiences*** by Nancy Duarte has been my required text for years at Stanford. Duarte moves beyond simply visual expertise (see her first book, *slide;ology*), but looks at the arc of a well-told story and well-crafted presentation. I see her sparkline as a breakthrough for all leaders struggling to present information in a compelling way to an audience who might resist.

10. ***Guide to Presentations*** by Mary Munter and Lynn Russell, from which the AIM framework is sourced. This is the oldest book on the list (and the only true textbook), but the AIM triangle has, for me, stood the test of time. It may be out of print by now, but definitely not out of use.

11. ***Bonus track:*** While I've not yet read it, I strongly encourage you to watch for my colleague Deb Gruenfeld's book, *Acting with Power*, due out in April 2020 from Crown Publishing Group/ Penguin Random House. Her work has become legendary at the GSB and I cannot wait to read her work on what business leaders can gain from studying the work that actors do.

BIBLIOGRAPHY

Aaker, Jennifer, and Smith, Andy. *The Dragonfly Effect: Quick, Effective, and Power-ful Ways to Use Social Media to Drive Social Change.* San Francisco, California: Jossey-Bass, a Wiley Imprint. 2010. ISBN: 978–0–470–61415–0.

Abrahams, Matthew. *Speaking Up Without Freaking Out: 50 Techniques for Confi-dent and Compelling Presenting.* Dubuque, Iowa: Kendall Hunt Publishing. 2010. ISBN: 978–1–4652–3738–5.

Alter, Cara Hale. *The Credibility Code: How to Project Competence When It Matters Most.* Meritus Books. 2012. ISBN: 978–0–9852656–0–1.

Anderson, Chris. *TED Talks: The Official TED Guide to Public Speaking.* New York, New York: Mariner Books. 2017. ISBN: 9780544634497.

Blake, Jenny. *Pivot: The Only Move That Matters Is Your Next One.* New York, New York: Penguin Random House. 2016, 2017. ISBN: 9781591848202.

Brosseau, Denise, and Kawasaki, Guy. *Ready to Be a Thought Leader?: How to Increase Your Influence, Impact, and Success.* Hoboken, New Jersey: John Wiley & Sons, Inc. 2013. ISBN: 978–1–118–79506–4.

Brown, Brené. *Daring Greatly: How the Courage to Be Vulnerable Transforms the Way We Live, Love, Parent, and Lead.* New York, New York: Gotham Books. 2012. ISBN: 978–1–592–40733–0.

Cabane, Olivia Fox. *The Charisma Myth: How Anyone Can Master the Art and Science of Personal Magnetism.* New York, New York. Portfolio/Penguin. 2012. ISBN: 978–1–59184–456–3.

Cain, Susan. *Quiet: The Power of Introverts in a World That Can't Stop Talking.* New York, New York: Broadway Paperbacks. 2012, 2013. ISBN: 978–0–307–35215–6.

Cuddy, Amy. *Presence: Bringing Your Boldest Self to Your Biggest Challenges.* New York, New York: Back Bay Books/Little, Brown and Company. 2015. ISBN: 978–0–316–25657–5.

Diemeyer, Daniel. *Reputation Rules: Strategies for Building Your Company's Most Valuable Asset.* New York, New York: McGraw-Hill Books. 2016. ISBN: 978–0–07–176374–5.

Duarte, Nancy. *Resonate: Present Visual Stories That Transform Audiences.* Hoboken, New Jersey: John Wiley & Sons, Inc. 2010. ISBN: 978–0–470–63201–7.

Duarte, Nancy. *slide:ology: The Art and Science of Creating Great Presentations.* Sebastopol, CA: O'reilly Media, Inc. 2008. ISBN: 978–0–596–52234–6.

Duarte, Nancy, and Sanchez, Patti. *Illuminate: Ignite Change Through Speeches, Stories, Ceremonies, and Symbols.* New York, New York: Portfolio/Penguin. 2016. ISBN: 978–1–101–98016–3.

Ertel, Chris, and Solomon, Lisa Kay. *Moments of Impact: How to Design Strategic Conversations That Accelerate Change.* New York, New York: Simon & Schuster. 2014. ISBN: 978–1–4516–9762–9.

Gallo, Carmine. *The Presentation Secrets of Steve Jobs: How to Be Insanely Great in Front of Any Audience.* New York, New York: McGraw-Hill. Gallo, Carmine, publisher. 2010. ISBN: 978–0–07–163608–7.

Grand, Adam, and Sandberg, Sheryl. *Originals: How Non-Conformists Move the World.* New York, New York: Penguin Books. 2016. ISBN: 9780143128854.

Grant, Adam. *Originals: How Non-Conformists Rule the World.* New York, New York: Penguin Books. 2016. ISBN: 97805254

Heath, Chip, and Heath, Dan. *Decisive: How to Make Better Choices in Life and Work.* New York, New York: Crown Business 2013. ISBN: 978–0–307–95639–2.

Heath, Chip, and Heath, Dan. *Made to Stick: Why Some Ideas Survive and Others Die.* New York, New York: Random House. 2007, 2008. ISBN: 978–4000–6428–1.

Heath, Chip, and Heath, Dan. *The Power of Moments: Why Certain Experiences Have Extraordinary Impact.* New York, New York: Simon & Schuster. 2017. ISBN: 978–1–5011–4776–0.

Heath, Chip, and Heath, Dan. *Switch: How to Change Things When Change Is Hard.* New York, New York: Crown Publishing Group. 2010. ISBN: 978–0–385–52875–7.

Heath, Kathryn, Flynn, Jill, and Davis Holt, Mary. "Women, Find Your Voice: Your Performance in Meetings Matters More Than You Think." *Harvard Business Review*, June 2014.

Ivester, Matt. *lol . . . OMG!: What Every Student Needs to Know About Online Reputation Management, Digital Citizenship and Cyberbullying.* Reno, Nevada: Serra Knight Publishing. 2011. ISBN: 978–1466242074.

Kay, Katty, and Shipman, Claire. "The Confidence Gap," *The Atlantic*, May 2014. http://www.theatlantic.com/magazine/archive/2014/05/theconfidencegap/359815/

Kinsey-Goman, Carol. *The Silent Language of Leaders: How Body Language Can Help—or Hurt—How You Lead*. San Francisco, California: Jossey-Bass/Wiley. 2011. ISBN: 978–0–470–87636–7.

Lamott, Anne. *Bird by Bird: Some Instructions on Writing and Life*. New York, New York: Anchor Books/Random House. 1995. ISBN: 978–0–385–48001–7.

Lewis, Mike. *When to Jump: When the Job You Have Isn't the Life You Want*. New York, New York: Henry Holt & Company. 2018. 9781250124210.

Lipp, Chris. *The Startup Pitch: A Proven Formula to Win Funding*. Palo Alto, California: Amazon. 2014. ISBN: 978–0–9911137–0–5.

Mehrabian, Albert. *Silent Messages*. Belmont, California: Wadsworth Publishing Company. 1981. ISBN: 0–534–00910–7.

Munter, Mary, and Russell, Lynn. *Guide to Presentations*. Upper Saddle River, New Jersey: Pearson Education, Inc. 2002. ISBN: 0–13–035132–6.

Nagle, Alice. *Savvy!: The Young Woman's Guide to Career Success*. Silicon Valley, California: Thorne Connelly Publishing. 2015. ISBN: 978–0–692–20220–3.

Neffinger, John, and Kohut, Matthew. *Compelling People: The Hidden Qualities That Make Us Influential*. New York, New York: Hudson Street Press/Penguin Group. 2013. ISBN: 978–1–59463–101–6.

Nussbaumer Knaflic, Cole. *Storytelling with Data: A Data Visualization Guide for Business Professionals*. Hoboken, New Jersey: John Wiley & Sons, Inc. 2015. ISBN: 9781119002253.

Osterwalder, Alexander, and Pigneur, Yves. *Business Model Generation*. Hoboken, New Jersey: John Wiley & Sons, Inc. 2010. ISBN: 978–0470–87641–7.

Peterson, Joel, and Kaplan, David A. *The Ten Laws of Trust: Building the Bonds That Make a Business Great*. New York, New York: AMACOM. 2016. ISBN: 9780814437452.

Pink, Daniel. *Drive: The Surprising Truth About What Motivates Us*. New York, New York. Riverhead Books. 2009. ISBN: 978–1–59448–884–9.

Russell, Lynn, and Munter, Mary. *Guide to Presentations*. 4th Edition. "Pearson 'Guide to' Series in Business Communication." Upper Saddle River, New Jersey: Pearson. 2013. ISBN: 0–13–035132–6.

Scott, Kim. *Radical Candor: Be a Kick-Ass Boss Without Losing Your Humanity*. New York, New York: St. Martin's Press. 2017. ISBN: 9781250103505.

Solomon, Lisa. *Design a Better Business: New Tools, Skills, and Mindset for Strategy and Innovation*. Hoboken, New Jersey: John Wiley & Sons. 2016. ISBN: 9781119272113.

Solomon, Lisa. *Moments of Impact: How to Design Strategic Conversations That Accelerate Change*. New York, New York: Simon & Schuster. 2014. ISBN: 978–1–4516–9762–9.

Weissman, Jerry. *In the Line of Fire: How to Handle Tough Questions . . . When It Counts*. Upper Saddle River, New Jersey: Pearson Education/Prentice Hall. 2005. ISBN: 0–13–185517–4.

Weissman, Jerry. *Presenting to Win: The Art of Telling Your Story*. Upper Saddle River, New Jersey: Pearson Education/Prentice Hall. 2003. ISBN: 0–13–046413–9.

ACKNOWLEDGMENTS

Other authors have told me the only people who will read this far in the book will be the people you remember to mention in the acknowledgments. My bigger fear is who I may leave out—those who may wend their way back here and not find their names. Let me apologize in advance if in my haste I may have failed to mention anybody. It's truly been an effort of my entire village to get this book written, published, and promoted. Thank you all!

First and foremost to my dedicated coauthor, Kara Levy, who believed we could do it and kept me going when I was ready to call it quits. She is a gifted writer, efficient editor, and remarkable partner. Moreover she is a talented communication coach on both written and spoken skills. I have gained so much from the gentle (and not so gentle) coaching she's given me during our work together. Without your partnership, this book would merely be a dream I never finished. It's now out in the world, allowing us to inspire even more leaders to communicate more effectively.

Clearly without the careful stewardship of my editor at Wiley, Jeanenne Ray, and project editor, Vicki Adang, this book would not have come to fruition. Their work was then picked up by Victoria Annlo, Dawn Kilgore, and Rebecca Taff. I'm grateful Wiley found me and was patient enough for me to get to the point in time when I could write a book. The entire team at Wiley deserves credit for the speed and accuracy of this publication.

Next we must thank the many past and present GSB colleagues who provided us access to their classrooms through this process. We've endeavored to name them as they were referenced: Matt Abrahams, Burt Alper, David Demarest, Allison Kluger, Raymond Nasr, David Schweidel, and Stephanie Soler. Behind the scenes I was given great support by the GSB administration, in particular Dean Jon Levin, and senior associate deans Madhav Rajan and Yossi Feinberg. Moreover, this work was informed by scores of coaches, lecturers, teaching assistants, and students too numerous to name. Thank you.

Further, I am grateful to those who read early drafts and were willing to provide feedback or endorsement, including Joel Peterson (who penned the foreword), Adam Grant, Kim Scott, Jon Levin, Nancy Duarte, Kylan Lundeen, Steve Mellas, Michael Roberto, Mike Lewis, Erin Uritus, John Tedstrom, Molly Epstein, and Tim Flood.

Along the way Sherry Shaker, Paul Huffstedler, Jacqulyne Law, Priyanka Basnyat, Gregory Holmes, Will Hanson, and Kiefer Hickman supported our efforts in a variety of ways large and small.

As of this writing, I've only just begun my new role at the Knight-Hennessy Scholars program but have already benefitted greatly from the guidance of John Hennessy and Derrick Bolton, and from the support of a remarkable team of professionals.

While my journey at Columbia was relatively short, its impact on my teaching and leadership was great. In particular I appreciate the specific insights from Becky Heino, Arabella Pollack, Kai Wright, and Tim Doocey, all of which helped to shape this book.

Within the field of Management Communication I am powerfully sustained by a network of colleagues at business schools across the globe who belong to MCA. My gratitude to Molly Epstein at Emory, Tim Flood at UNC Chapel Hill, Kimberly Pace at Vanderbilt, Kara Blackburn at MIT, and Evelyn Williams at Georgetown, and to all the MCA members who've inspired me to share generously. And my career started at NYU under the mentorship of the legendary Irv

Schenkler; he took a chance on me in the spring of 2003, which led to a career I treasure.

My love of writing and speaking stretches way back in my life. So many great educators challenged me—in particular, Mary Rose Rohr, Kay Hoffman, Juleen Stecklein, David Wessling, Fr. Blaine Burkey, OFM Cap, and Ronald Q. Frederickson. My foundation in Kansas contributes to my own teaching and writing to this day.

The Battery in San Francisco served as one of my most productive refuges for writing this manuscript. I hope to return there to celebrate its publication!

Many friends have supported me throughout this journey, including fellow authors like Barbara Bryson, Matthew Lambert, Chris Lipp, Tina Seelig, Chip Heath, Jennifer Aaker, Jeff Pfeffer, Kai Wright, Mike Lewis, and Michael Roberto. Seeing what you've accomplished has motivated me to (at last) join your club.

Finally, I began by dedicating this book to my husband and children, so I end by thanking them once more. They've blessed me with solitude to write and edit, and with joyful distraction when I needed a break. Joshua, Roma, Toby, and Ken, you are the wind beneath my wings and the motivation for doing all that I do. Thank you so much for allowing me this journey.

ABOUT THE AUTHORS

JD Schramm founded and led the Mastery in Communication Initiative at Stanford's Graduate School of Business, where he's served as lecturer in Organizational Behavior since 2007. He helped grow the communication offerings at the GSB from none in 2007 to more than 20 sections of elective courses in the 2019. He co-founded the LOWKeynotes program, where students work with a professional communication coach to conceive, prepare, and deliver a nine-minute TED-like talk to a packed audience of their peers. He currently serves as the inaugural director of the King Global Leadership Program for the Knight-Hennessy Scholars at Stanford University while continuing to teach graduate communication courses.

JD Schramm has spoken at TED and TEDx events and has coached scores of others to do the same. His writing has appeared in the *Washington Post,* the *San Francisco Chronicle*, the *Huffington Post*, and HBR Online. A sought-out speaker and trainer, he's worked with firms and groups including the Aspen Institute Presidential Fellows for Community College Excellence, Qualtrics, YPO, Facebook, Breakline, Jane Street Financial, GenenTech, Ciena, AQR Capital, Adams Street Partners, and Google. JD is an active member of the LGBTQ community, particularly focused on inclusion efforts within higher education and communities of worship. He's an advocate for suicide prevention, foster care services, and HIV/AIDS research.

During the 2018–2019 school year he served as the faculty director for Columbia University's Career Design Lab in San Francisco, an innovative West Coast presence for Columbia. Schramm holds his Ed.D. in higher education leadership from the University of Pennsylvania, his MBA from NYU's Stern School of Business, and his BFA in theater from Emporia State University in Kansas. He and his husband, Rev. Ken Daigle, make their home in San Francisco raising three very active children.

Kara Levy is an executive communication and leadership coach based in the San Francisco Bay Area. She began her coaching career at the Stanford Graduate School of Business, where she was an early member of the Mastery in Communication Initiative and spent nearly a decade in a variety of coaching roles, including the LOWKeynotes and India Innovation Growth programs. Since then, Kara's coaching and trainings have offered thousands of leaders the tools to speak more confidently off the cuff; to become faster and better writers, more competent storytellers, and more empathetic and efficient problem-solvers; and to develop executive presence that feels authentic to them. Her collaborations in Silicon Valley range from household names like Facebook and Salesforce to unique startups just beginning to craft their company cultures. Kara holds an MFA in fiction writing from Columbia University and lives in San Francisco with her daughter.

INDEX

Note: Page references in *italics* refer to figures.